W9-AUS-236

LITTLE THINGS MATTER

100 Ways to Improve Your Life Today

This book is being given to

_____

because I care about you.

_____

LITTLE
THINGS
MATTER

100 Ways to
Improve Your Life Today

W. Todd Smith

SUCCESS|BOOKS®
Lake Dallas, Texas

Dedication

This book is lovingly dedicated to my family who
have filled my home with love and laughter
and been a source of encouragement throughout my life:

Joy, my wife and best friend,
who for 25 years has believed in my potential,
allowed me to dream,
encouraged me in each of my endeavors,
and supported me in the writing of this book.

Gerrid, my first born,
who has been my best student
and now my partner and wise counselor.

Danielle, my eldest daughter,
whose smile and positive spirit
have provided me with hope and reason
to pursue my dreams.

Jake, my teenager,
who will no doubt surpass
my own success with his talent and
desire to achieve great things.

Hannah, the sparkler,
who assists me with my blog and
keeps our home filled with
wonder and excitement.

Lois, my mom,
who has poured her love and encouragement
into my life since the day I was born.

Don, my dad,
who is the most unselfish person I know
and who has always been there when I needed him.

Acknowledgements

Writing a book is a challenging endeavor—one not to be embarked upon without the loyal support and encouragement of family and friends.

I want to especially mention those who have worked diligently beside me for these many months:

My LTM Team: Joshua Cearbaugh, Gerrid Smith, Hannah Smith, Joy Smith, Jake Smith, Danielle Cearbaugh, Barry Smith and Jessica Smith have been with me from the very beginning as we gave birth to this book and throughout the long months while it came into being. Their advice and participation have been invaluable.

My Collaborator: Ronnie Weston has been instrumental in helping me formulate the lessons for this book. I could not have completed this monumental task without her assistance.

My Editorial Team: Ronnie Weston, Robin Hendricks, Mary Erickson, and Denise Haley have given unselfishly of their time and expertise to make this book the best it can be.

My Brand Manager: Jessica Smith who gave freely of her time to work with the designers on the design of the book.

My Advisors: Darren Hardy and Mary Erickson who have provided me with wise counsel as I have journeyed through this process.

My Supporters: I'm grateful to the many people who found time in their busy schedules to read and comment on my growing manuscript. Their observations, remarks, and suggestions contributed considerably to this published work. I want to express my thanks to Mark Davy, Stuart Johnson, Matt Otto, Jack Smith, Nancy Smith, Eddie Stone, and my LTM team.

Brian Tracy: For his support in writing the Foreword to this book.

My Artist: Lily Zaryan took my ideas and designed an attractive cover.

My Publisher: Reed Bilbray and his team took all our efforts and produced the finished product you have in your hands.

Foreword

It is a pleasure for me to be able to write this foreword for Todd Smith's wonderful book, "Little Things Matter."

Todd has discovered and eloquently written about one of the greatest success secrets of all time, "for things to get better, you must get better."

Every great success is the result of hundreds and even thousands of little efforts that no one ever sees or appreciates. The interesting fact is that the law of probabilities determines your success as much as anything else. The more that you do the things that other successful people do, over and over, the more probable it is that you will get the success that successful people enjoy. It is not a miracle. It is not luck; it is merely law, the law of probabilities.

Interestingly enough, when it comes to success, achievement, and wealth creation, nature has no favorites. Nature doesn't really care. Nature is neutral. Nature operates on the iron law of the universe, the law of cause and effect. If you put in the causes, you will eventually get out the effects. And if you don't, you won't.

I have spoken to 5,000 audiences in 56 countries over a 30-year career in professional speaking and writing. I have produced 52 books that have been published in as many as 38 languages and which are sold in more than 50 countries. What I have learned is that you can never know exactly what thing it is that you do that will lead to your success. But if you do more and more of the hundred strategies taught in this book, you dramatically increase the likelihood that you will achieve everything you want in life.

Perhaps the most important mental law I have ever discovered is the law of correspondence. This law says that your outer world is a mirror-image reflection of your inner world. If you want to change anything in your outer world, your health, relationships, income or success of any kind, you must first begin by changing yourself on the inside.

They say that everyone wants to go to heaven, but nobody wants to die. Everyone wants to be successful, but very few people want to put in the many months and years of hard work necessary to achieve it. But you cannot accomplish something on the outside that you have not prepared yourself for on the inside. That is why we say that, "To achieve something that you have never achieved before, you must become someone that you have never been before."

We are living in a turbulent and challenging world today. And if anything, the achievement of the success you desire will be more difficult and challenging in the months and years ahead than it has ever been before. You need everything possible going for you if you are going to survive and thrive in the "new reality" in which we live today.

This book gives you a series of ideas, methods, techniques and strategies that you can use immediately to take control of your life and get better results in everything you do.

The most important quality of successful people is "action-orientation." When they hear an idea or get an opportunity, they move fast. They develop a "sense of urgency." They are constantly in motion. They are proactive rather than passive. As a result, they take and keep complete control of their destiny.

You must do the same. Each time you get an idea for an action you can take as you read this book, implement it immediately. Don't delay. Don't procrastinate. Don't put it off until another day, or until everything is "just right." Your future destiny is in your hands, and by following the wonderful ideas in this book, you can step on the accelerator of your potential and accomplish more in the weeks and months ahead than most people will accomplish in many years.

Brian Tracy

Preface

Whether you want to become the world's best parent, develop into your company's most valued employee, be a top-producing salesperson, or the owner of your own successful business, the habits you develop and choices you make—no matter how insignificant they seem at the time—will define the level of success you achieve.

Jim Rohn, who has been hailed as one of the most influential thinkers of our time and whose teachings have been a source of guidance for me throughout my career, said, *"For your life to get better you must get better."*

Far too often I've observed that people focus exclusively on processes or strategies to achieve their goals without giving serious consideration to their personal attributes. In other words, they never ask themselves who they need to become to achieve their goals.

Brian Tracy, author of more than 50 books and audio programs on personal achievement and whose teachings have also had a profound influence on my life, said, *"To achieve something that you have never achieved before, you must become someone that you have never been before."*

Bound within the covers of this book are 100 short, action-driven lessons that can help you become the person you need to be to achieve both your personal and professional goals.

Regardless of race or age, position or education, you have the chance to grow and develop skills, to build positive relationships, to create an attractive personality, to reach your goals, and to enjoy a happy and fulfilling life.

I hope that as you read and consider these LITTLE THINGS, you will become excited about developing yourself. As you begin implementing these lessons into your daily life, you will experience more energy and a stronger motivation, new courage and inspiration, renewed hope and greater confidence. Growing and becoming a better person is one of the most rewarding feelings you will ever experience.

Thanks for giving me the opportunity to share the lessons I've learned. I hope they make as big a difference in your life as they have in mine.

Wishing you success in achieving your personal and professional best,

W. Todd Smith

> **Success is not something you pursue.**
> **What you pursue eludes you.**
> **Success is something you attract**
> **by the person you become.**
> Jim Rohn

How to Read This Book

How many LITTLE THINGS matter?

Twenty-five years ago, I started making a list and today it contains close to 1000 LITTLE THINGS. This book includes 100 of them.

As you read the lessons, keep two questions in mind:

- Which of the LITTLE THINGS are you not doing?
- Which of those that you are doing, could you do better and with greater consistency?

The lessons I selected for this book are those that can be applied to both your personal life and professional life. This information, when acted upon, will help you become a better parent and role model for your children; will bring more depth to your valued relationships; will increase people's respect for you and your influence in the community, and will help you achieve whatever level of professional success you desire. I believe that, if you apply these lessons to any part of your life, you will see measureable results almost immediately.

Some of the LITTLE THINGS will feel natural and come easy for you; some will require pushing yourself outside your comfort zone. Some will challenge your current beliefs; some will provide "Aha" moments. Some may be life changing, and some you'll be tempted to dismiss as insignificant. Don't allow yourself to think that one of these LITTLE THINGS doesn't matter. They all matter.

When you read a lesson about a subject you think you know well, ask yourself, *"Being honest with myself, how am I doing on this point?"* As you contemplate your answer, review the Little Things Matter (LTM) Challenge at the end of each lesson for ideas about taking your skill to the next level. The best of the best got there by being the best at the LITTLE THINGS. When a new concept is presented to you, use your personal initiative to start small and take the first step. With each small step you take, your confidence grows. Every great success story begins with the first step, and then another.

Most importantly, be intentional as you implement this principle—*Little Things Matter*—into your everyday actions, being mindful of Jim Rohn's cautionary advice, "*What is easy to do is easy not to do.*" The key is to practice these LITTLE THINGS consistently so they become habits.

Just a note to my international readers: Having lived my entire life in the United States, my observations and recommendations are distinctive to American society. Readers from other countries or cultures may find that a few lessons offer a different perspective than their customs. For the most part, however, the LITTLE THINGS are reflective of our globally interconnected society.

While you can dive into any one of the LITTLE THINGS, I suggest that you start with Number 1 and work your way through the book, one lesson at a time. Regardless, just have fun and enjoy learning about a new way of thinking.

> **The elevator to success is not running.**
> **Take the stairs.**
> Author unknown

Table of Contents

The Extended Todd Smith Family

Front Row: Jessica, Jake, Hannah, Danielle

Back Row: Gerrid, Todd, Titus, Joy, Joshua

Introduction

Meet the Author—W. Todd Smith

Todd Smith is a family man as well as an entrepreneur. He has been married to Joy, his high-school sweetheart, for 25 years. They have been blessed with four remarkable children whom Joy has homeschooled. Since Todd works out of his home office, they have been able to forge a unique relationship as a family. Recently his oldest daughter Danielle presented him with his first grandson—Titus Joshua. Todd still can't believe he's old enough to be called *Gramps*.

As a dynamic entrepreneur for 30 years, Todd Smith has enjoyed extraordinary personal and professional success.

However, he did not get off to a good start. Because of a lack of finances, college wasn't an option. Todd's first job after graduating from high school was rather nondescript. He was a ditch digger laying cable for the local cable company, making six bucks an hour. That job lasted only five months because the cable company had financial troubles. Then he became a package runner for UPS during the Christmas holidays.

Being laid off from two jobs within six months was an awakening experience for this teenager. It was at this time that his older brother Jack invited him to move to Chicago and start a silk-screening business. He quickly accepted the invitation and the challenge, packed up his few belongings, drove to Chicago, and took up residence in Jack's guest bedroom.

Over the next four-and-a-half years what started as a small business in a garage became one of the most successful businesses of its type in the Chicago area.

At age 23, they sold that business and Todd became a Realtor™. It was at this time that he started devouring everything that he could he get his hands on in the personal and professional success category. In addition to learning from the top teachers in the area of human development and personal achievement, he observed people's behavior and tried to distinguish the characteristics and skills of those at the top compared to everyone else in their fields.

As he continued to learn and grow, he felt that something was missing. Most of these great teachers talked about the <u>big</u> things people need to do to succeed—such as setting goals, employing discipline, and having a positive attitude—but his gut told him something was still missing. He saw too many people doing these <u>big</u> things, yet still falling short of reaching their goals.

Then one day, while listening to a story called "The Point System" told by Brian Tracy, the missing pieces came together for Todd.

Brian described two salesmen going head-to-head in an imaginary sales contest. The winner needed to earn 100 points. Both men were well groomed (worth 5 points) and appropriately dressed (worth 8 points). They both kept appointments and followed up as requested (worth 4 points). Each was knowledgeable about their products (worth 6 points) and gave remarkable presentations (worth 10 points). With the evaluations nearly complete, the salesmen were tied at 99 points each. One more factor was taken into account—their pens. One used a *Cross* pen throughout his presentation (worth 2 points); the other used a *Bic* pen, which had no point value.

The salesman with the *Cross* pen won the contest. One LITTLE THING made the difference between winning and losing a sale. One LITTLE THING, seemingly insignificant, separated one salesman from the other. **One LITTLE THING mattered.**

Todd began applying the *little-things-matter* concept to his real estate career and the results were almost immediate. He asked himself this question: *"What are the things I could do that would ultimately affect a seller's decision as to whether or not they would select me to market their home?"*

Here's Todd's personal account of his plan that brought him success and eventually developed into this book.

How Todd Created His Brand—in His Own Words

First, I made a list of the fundamental things that I should do. Realizing that these qualities were the same as those my competitors would list, I needed to take it a step further. I had to be creative and stretch my mind and think of all the LITTLE THINGS that would give me the edge.

Here's a glimpse of some of the LITTLE THINGS that gave me the competitive advantage:

- I was very friendly in all of my communications.
- I wore a suit every day even when it was hot.
- I made sure my tie was in style and the proper length.

- I kept my shoes shined.
- I bought a Cadillac that I could not afford because I needed to brand myself as being successful.
- I carried a pager and returned all my calls within one hour.
- I arrived for my appointments five to ten minutes early to mentally prepare for the appointments. I rang the doorbell at the exact time I was supposed to be there. I was never late.
- I greeted people with a smile, a friendly greeting, and a firm handshake.
- I made equal eye contact with both the husband and wife throughout our conversations.
- I asked questions about items in their homes to show I cared about their interests.
- I introduced myself to their children and called them by their names.
- I petted their dogs or cats even though I was allergic to most animals.
- I looked for something about which I could sincerely pay them a compliment.
- I used an attractive, high-quality leather presentation book.
- I told them with a confident tone that, if they were not completely satisfied with my efforts to sell their home, they could cancel the listing agreement within 24 hours.
- I always sent a thank-you note after my presentation.
- Of course, I never left home without my Cross pen.

By applying what I learned, I earned more than $250,000 my first year. During the next three years, as I listened to more self-development tapes, read more books, and observed other successful people, my list grew longer. I was constantly thinking about and looking for the LITTLE

THINGS that would improve my personal brand and help me stand out from my competitors.

One way was to become humble and vulnerable. I learned a lot from my mistakes. When a home-seller selected a competitor over me, I thanked the home-seller for giving me the opportunity to present my services and requested feedback and constructive criticism.

Not only did I focus on the LITTLE THINGS that mattered, but I also began to master the LITTLE THINGS by striving for excellence. As I mastered each LITTLE THING, my value to the market grew exponentially and so did my income.

Within four-and-a-half years, I became one of the nation's top-selling Realtors, selling more than 115 homes a year and earning the distinction of being one of the youngest Realtors ever inducted into the RE/MAX™ Hall of Fame.

Tired of the long cold Chicago winters, I moved to Florida at age 28 and started my own sales and marketing business. By applying the *Little Things Matter* way of thinking to my new career, I've enjoyed a level of success I had never thought I would achieve. During the last 20 years, my business has generated more than $1 billion in sales and has paid me $23 million in commissions.

Little Things Matter has become a way of thinking that I've applied to every part of my life—developing my career, enjoying a marriage of 25 years, parenting four children, volunteering in the community, coaching children's sports teams, and teaching other entrepreneurs.

The journey hasn't ended. I continue to look for the LITTLE THINGS I am not doing and the things I can do better. I hope that by the time you finish reading this book you will decide to join me on this journey.

Now as I write this book, after 25 years of testing and trying, the evidence is undeniable—*Little Things Matter.*

> **All successful people, men and women, are big dreamers.**
> **They imagine what their future could be, ideal in every respect,**
> **and then they work every day**
> **toward their distant vision, that goal or purpose.**
> Brian Tracy

1. A New Attitude for a New Day

If you want to enjoy greater success, you must put the past behind you and focus on your future. You can move beyond your failures and disappointments to create a new, amazing life. I'm a firm believer in Napoleon Hill's famous quotation: *"What the mind of man can conceive and believe, it can achieve."* Attitude is everything.

Here is what I know from *failing* my way to the top. If you continue to dwell upon your past failures, losses, and disappointments, you cannot advance your life forward. Spending time thinking about them will have a negative effect on your emotions and immobilize you from taking action.

You have no doubt experienced this negative feeling. Everyone has at some time or another. In fact, anyone who has been willing to venture out of his or her comfort zone has experienced huge disappointment and failure.

Where do you stand today? Are you still haunted by the past? Are you preoccupied with the memory of negative experiences? Here's what Jim Rohn, one of my favorite teachers, had to say:

> *We must not beat ourselves to death with past mistakes, faults, failures, and losses. The greatest opportunity today brings with it the opportunity to begin the process of change.*

As you begin this series of lessons on the LITTLE THINGS that can lead you to a better life, remember that today is a new day.

Learn From the Past

- **Acknowledge your mistakes.** When you make a mistake, accept responsibility for the decision that led to the mistake. Denial leads to repetition of the same mistakes and sends your self-image into a downward spiral.

- **Identify what drove you to make the mistake.** Often mistakes can reveal a new part of you. Address them and make needed changes. Don't be discouraged if this process takes five minutes, a couple of hours, or perhaps even days.

- **Don't stay mired in the muck.** Holding on to disappointment can cause you to be bitter and depressed. Instead, learn from your disappointments and get excited about becoming the person you need to be to achieve your goals and live the life you desire.

In the words of Irish poet and author Oscar Wilde: *"What seems to us as bitter trials are often blessings in disguise."*

Create Your Future

- **Maintain a positive attitude.** Look at challenges as opportunities to become a better person. The times when I have grown the most have followed my major failures. I'm convinced you can work through any challenge that comes your way if you look at it as a chance to improve.

- **Develop self-control.** This will require a conscious effort. Every time I catch myself thinking about one of my failures, I have a firm conversation with myself: *"I can't change what has happened. I've learned all I can learn. I refuse to think about it any longer!"* Then using self-control, I change my thought process.

- **Don't compare yourself with others**. No matter what you have experienced, there are people who have had it better than you, and there are people who have had it far worse. I've seen some very gifted people miss golden opportunities because they were concerned with what other people were doing and how they were getting ahead. Concentrate on your own growth potential.

LTM Challenge

Draw a line in the sand to separate your past from your future and begin focusing 100 percent of your emotional energy on creating a fulfilling life. If you truly know what it is you want and are willing to do what it takes to achieve it, you can live the life of your dreams.

> **Dwelling on the events of yesterday causes you to miss the fun and excitement of today and the anticipation of what tomorrow may bring.**

2. What's Important to You?

As I have studied success and experienced it first-hand, there is absolutely no doubt in my mind that the starting point to living a more successful and fulfilling life is to positively know what's important to you. You must identify the things you value most.

When I was struggling to become an entrepreneur, I was taught that the first step to achieving success is to have a strong desire.

However, throughout my career, I have coached hundreds of aspiring entrepreneurs who wanted something so much *they could taste it*. Or, at least that's what they told me. Yet when it came time to employ the discipline needed to achieve their goals, many of them opted out; they wouldn't exercise the necessary discipline.

Another prime example of desire not being enough lies in the real estate profession. First-year Realtor dropout rates are as high as 80 percent. Don't you think these men and women had a strong desire to become successful Realtors when they first started out?

What happened to their desire? Why did they fail to follow through? Answer: What they desired was not important enough for them to do the things required to achieve their objectives.

Let me encourage you to stop spending time pursuing things you simply desire or <u>think</u> are important. Instead, identify the things that you <u>know</u> are important. It's a small but critical distinction. Far too many people waste large periods of their lives climbing mountains only to realize, when they get to the top, they climbed the wrong ones. Internationally respected author and leadership consultant Stephen Covey speaks to this:

> *How different our lives are when we really know what is deeply important to us, and, keeping that picture in mind, we manage ourselves each day to be and to know what really matters most.*

LTM Challenge

Make a list of things that are important to you. Then prioritize that list, identifying the most important one, followed by the second, and so on. As you make this list, be honest. Don't put something at the top of the list if it really isn't your Number 1 priority.

You can say, *"My family is really important to me,"* but if you're traveling two weeks a month and working 60 or 70 hours a week, your actions speak louder than your words. What truly are your priorities?

If you are going to move your life forward, you can't play games with yourself and pretend things are different than they really are. When you complete this exercise, you will have a prioritized list of things that are most important for you to achieve.

Please stop and do this exercise. The lessons that follow will not bring the same value to your life if you have not completed this challenge.

Desire alone is not enough to break through the obstacles that lie in your path. What you pursue must be something that, deep down in your inner being, is very important to you.

---

3. Believe You Can

Success requires a can-do attitude like the little blue engine proved in the classic children's book, *The Little Engine That Could.* In 1930, Watty Piper personified a small engine that truly believed she could pull a long train over a steep hill.

Constantly repeating her mantra—*I think I can! I think I can! I think I can!* —she succeeded. Very soon the train was over the hill and going down the other side.

How can you be more like the little blue engine and reach your potential? Your first step is to wipe out limiting beliefs. We all harbor them. John Assaraf and Murray Smith reported in their book *The Answer*, that by the time children reach their 17th birthday they have heard *"No you can't"* 150,000 times and *"Yes you can!"* only 5,000 times. Combining mistakes and failures with a focus on faults and weaknesses in an environment of negative people creates a rich breeding ground for self-doubt.

Perhaps the most common of all limiting beliefs is the idea that you can't reach a certain level of success. On a success scale of 1-10, you may think you can make it to a 7 but not a 10. If someone else has reached a 10, why can't you? Really! Think about it. Why can't you?

Once the seed of a limiting belief is planted in the mind, it's generally fertilized with negative self-talk. When the internal dialogue really gets going, you say things like, *"I can't do anything right,"* or *"I could never do that,"* or *"I can't make good decisions."* These statements are all false, yet you allow yourself to think they are true.

Many of these self-limiting statements are simply excuses for something someone would rather not do or is fearful of doing. For instance, someone says, *"I could never stand in front of people and give a presentation."* Unless they literally can't speak, they are deceiving themselves by saying they can't do it.

The more you make these types of false statements, the more you will believe them. Soon you'll experience a downward spiral of negativity.

To get beyond the barriers of self-limiting beliefs, ask yourself this question: If I were paid a million dollars to figure out a way to do a task, could I do it? If your answer is yes, then with focus and hard work you are capable of eliminating negative beliefs.

In your quest to achieve your goals, be confident in who you are and in your abilities. Don't allow self-defeating thoughts to limit your opportunities or prevent you from searching for solutions. Reach for the stars! Give all you've got and don't look back.

LTM Challenge

Starting today be aware of the times when you say, *"I can't"* or any other self-limiting statement. When you find yourself saying such negative things, immediately challenge yourself to do the very thing you said you couldn't do. As you begin doing the very things you said you could not do, your confidence will grow and you will feel great about the person you are becoming.

> **If you believe you can, you can.**
> **If you believe you can't, you can't.**

4. Become the Best at What You Do

Imagine if you were the best at what you do: the best salesperson, the best student, the best dad, the best mom, the best cashier, the best company president, the best insurance agent. THE BEST. How would your life change? How would you feel about yourself? What effects would you being the best have on those around you?

You can be the best at whatever you do as long as becoming the best is truly important to you. This doesn't mean thinking, *"Yeah, I think it would be cool if I were the best at what I do."* Or, *"Of course, I'd like to be the best. Who wouldn't?"* While most people might say they would like to be the best at what they do, very few people (less than 1 percent) are willing to do what is required to be the best. The best of the best are the best for a reason.

First, you must identify the LITTLE THINGS that, if done correctly, will allow you to perform at the highest level. The next step is to strive for excellence and master those LITTLE THINGS, measuring and refining what you do along the way.

After deciding to become a Realtor, I strived for excellence to master the LITTLE THINGS required to be a success. Day after day, week after week, and year after year, I continued to refine everything—from the scripts used, to the hours I made cold calls. I focused on every detail—from the paper used for my presentations to remembering the name of my client's dog.

After four years of making daily refinements, I perfected my craft reaching the top 1 percent of 1 percent of all the Realtors in the nation. I applied this same way of thinking to my sales and training career over the last 20 years and once again became one of the best at what I do.

Just as Olympic athletes master the fundamentals of their sports, so does anyone who wants to be the best of the best. They are the ones who work the hardest at mastering the littlest of things. As Napoleon Hill so aptly advised,

> *Have a well-developed sense of observation regarding the small details and know your craft from the smallest detail to the greatest.*

As you begin to implement the things you learn, stretch yourself every day to do your very best. Push yourself harder than you have ever pushed before. Regardless of your age, education or background, if you strive for excellence to be the very best at what you do, you will make great strides in becoming the person you need to be to get what you want.

LTM Challenge

What is really important to you? If you want to be a great parent, discover the LITTLE THINGS that great parents do; then work on those things each day. If you want to reach the top of your career, then identify the LITTLE THINGS that the top performers in your field do and then strive to master them.

As you strive for excellence to do your best, make sure you measure your progress. You will never be the best of the best if you are not measuring and refining your progress. As you see yourself making measurable progress, be sure to recognize yourself for even the smallest accomplishment.

Get excited and consider the possibilities of becoming the best at what you do!

> **To be the best at what you do, you must push and stretch yourself to do what others are unwilling to do. The best of the best are the best for a reason.**

5. Listen to and Control Your Self-Talk

Guess who's the Number 1 person you communicate with on a daily basis? It's you! Our minds are in a constant state of self-talk. These internal conversations characterize how we view the world and influence every part of our lives: relationships, achievements, attitude and, ultimately, our degree of happiness.

If this internal dialogue is negative—focusing on faults, mistakes, weaknesses, insecurities, or fears—it will be virtually impossible to feel good about yourself and advance your life forward.

Furthermore, sustained negative thinking can have a detrimental effect on your health and overall quality of life. If, on the other hand, your self-talk is positive—concentrating on your strengths, blessings, successes, and opportunities—your self-image will be strong and vibrant. Your obstacles won't seem insurmountable and, as a whole, your life will become more enjoyable and gratifying.

The great news is that you can control what you think. You can replace any negative thought with a more positive and productive affirmation. You'll soon find that the process gets easier with sustained practice.

The first step toward improving your thoughts is to become aware of your internal conversations and really listen to your inner voice.

- Are your thoughts positive or negative?
- Do they lift you up or do they bring you down?
- Do they inspire or do they impede?

Be aware of this internal dialogue and its content; make sure it stays positive. When it becomes negative, take a few minutes to analyze the underlying reasons for your pessimistic thinking.

If you catch yourself thinking negatively, you can stop your thought process mid-stream by literally saying to yourself, *"Stop!"* Saying this aloud has power; you're bound to notice the frequency and circumstances of these destructive internal conversations.

Every time I catch myself thinking about one of my failures, faults or mistakes, I have a firm conversation with myself. Then using my self-control, I change the subject. I confess that I may have to repeat this self-talk technique 20 times before I finally stop thinking about a major mistake or failure. But, as with every challenge I have faced thus far in my life, I have not allowed it to negatively impact my overall outlook.

LTM Challenge

Let me encourage you to start being aware of your self-talk. Determine which conversations are helpful and which ones are harmful. Be mindful that your internal conversations not only affect how you view yourself, but also how you react and respond to others.

Remember, we all make mistakes. We all have setbacks. We all experience failures. The key is to learn from every experience and use our self-control to stop thinking about them. It is only then that we can take positive steps to achieve our personal and professional best.

> **You can't control your life
> if you don't control your thoughts.**

6. Choose Your Friends Wisely

When I was a kid growing up, my mom gave me all sorts of advice. Today I can still hear her saying, *"Todd, choose your friends carefully. Don't get mixed up with the wrong group."* Mom knew children were easily influenced by their peers and that if I ran with the wrong crowd they'd have a negative influence on my life.

Mom's lesson holds true for children, teens, college students, and adults. It is well documented that our fundamental beliefs and attitudes are greatly influenced by the people we allow into our lives. If we associate with people who gossip, we are likely to gossip. If we are around people who swear and use inappropriate language, we're likely to exhibit the same behavior.

After 25 years of research, Dr. David McClelland of Harvard University concluded that the choice of a negative "reference group" was in itself enough to condemn a person to failure and underachievement in life.
Your associations are some of the most powerful factors in determining who you become and what you accomplish in your life. As an example, if you hang out with pessimistic people who are critical of you, their negative comments will likely impact how you view your abilities and your self-image.

Almost 20 years ago I heard Jim Rohn say, *"You will become the combined average of the five people you hang around the most. You will have their combined attitude, health, and income."*

At first I questioned whether this could be true. Today, I know it is undeniably accurate. Recognizing this truth, how do we use it to our advantage? It's simple. If we want to advance our lives personally and professionally, we must associate with people who will have a positive influence on our lives.

Do you play sports? How about board and card games? Do you notice how you step up your game when you play with better players? When we associate with others who have a greater skill set or have achieved more, we are challenged. It brings out the best in us and inspires us to do better. Observing and modeling someone's positive example will help us reach new heights.

We're not just talking sports and games here. This applies to everything we do. Surrounding ourselves with optimistic and uplifting people has a direct effect on our demeanor, confidence level, and performance.

LTM Challenge

Take ten minutes right now to think about the people who you spend time with on a regular basis-—at home, in the workplace, and in a social context. Who are they? Which ones radiate a positive influence? Which ones transmit a negative influence?

- If some of your friends exert a negative influence, begin to slowly reduce the amount of time you spend in those relationships.

- If your family members say negative and discouraging things to you, schedule time to have a conversation. Help them understand how their statements are damaging, and ask them to focus on encouraging you rather than tearing you down.

- If your workplace is filled with negative people, find a new place to work. Life is too short to spend it in a negative environment.

> **Whether you are consciously aware of it or not,
> everyone you associate with on a regular basis
> is influencing your life.
> The question is whether they are a good or bad influence.**

7. Strengthen Your Personal Initiative

Your personal initiative is the spark that initiates your productive actions. Without personal initiative, you cannot be successful.

Napoleon Hill talked about personal initiative at length in his 9th Principle of Success. He said, *"Success is something you must achieve without someone telling you what to do or why you should do it."*

Success comes to those who are proactive. Instead of drifting through life doing only what is required, successful people do the extra things that give direction to their goals and bring more meaning to their lives. No one told Fred Smith to start FedEx; he started it using his own personal initiative. No one told Sergey Brin and Larry Page why they should start Google; they did it using their own personal initiative. No one pushed me every day to do the things that were required of me to achieve my goals; it was the consistent use of my personal initiative that allowed me to achieve them.

No matter what your goal is—becoming a remarkable parent, one of your company's most valued employees, an outstanding athlete, a top-producing salesperson, or the owner of your own business—if you are going to be successful, you must use your personal initiative to do the LITTLE THINGS required of you to succeed. It won't happen any other way.

Personal initiative is more than a fundamental requirement to achieving your goals; it's about taking time to do the LITTLE THINGS that make your life and the lives of others, both at work and at home, more enjoyable.

It's doing the simple things like picking up your dirty clothes, washing the windows, or emptying the overflowing trashcan. It's taking three minutes to clean the coffee mugs in the sink at the office. It's taking time to express your genuine gratitude to someone who did something for you. It's offering to help a friend in need.

In a sense, your personal initiative is noticing and being aware of the things that need to be done without being asked.

I firmly believe that the only way you will have personal initiative to do big things is to strengthen it by first doing the LITTLE THINGS. Every big success is made up a great number of little successes, each requiring personal initiative. Many are so insignificant that you will be the only person who notices. But, in the end, isn't that what matters? After all, it is you who has the deep yearning in your heart to achieve a goal; you're the one responsible for taking action and making decisions; and, you're the one who can change course if required.

The use of personal initiative has more benefits than meet the eye.

- **Become respected**. People who use their personal initiative are well regarded and have greater influence.

- **Build self-esteem**. No other method for building self-esteem is more effective than using your personal initiative to do the LITTLE THINGS you know you should do.

- **Advance your career**. People who consistently use their personal initiative to advance their careers are those who are at the top of the pay scale in their profession.

LTM Challenge

This is your opportunity to step up your game and distinguish yourself from the growing number of apathetic people. This is your chance to use your unique talents and skills to achieve the things that are important to you. Don't let the lethargic environment around you keep you from stretching yourself to be your very best.

Start by doing the things that require personal initiative. As you build your confidence in doing these LITTLE Things, stretch yourself to do the bigger things. Continue this process and allow each success to build upon the prior one.

> **Now is the time to put your life in gear**
> **and go conquer your dreams.**

8. Create a Well-Developed Action Plan

Just as you would not be successful in building a home without a set of blueprints, it's doubtful you would be successful in achieving any significant goal without an action plan. A well-developed action plan clarifies everything you need to do to achieve your goal, outlines a prioritized sequence of steps, and serves as a method for measuring your progress.

I would like to share with you two personal examples that demonstrate the connection between a well-thought-out, written action plan and the achievement of a specific goal.

My Plan to Earn $400,000

In January of 1989, I set a goal to earn $400,000 by selling residential real estate. In reviewing my sales numbers from the previous year, I determined that if I wanted to make $400,000, I would need to sell 117 homes at an average sales price of $115,000.

My first step was to concentrate on identifying potential home sellers. Based upon my previous year's prospecting results, I would have to meet with 252 prospective sellers over the next 52 weeks to reach my goal, translating into five appointments a week or one per business day. My record-keeping from the previous year helped me assess how many phone calls I needed to make each day in order to schedule one appointment.

By the end of the year, I had met with 250 prospective sellers—two short of my goal, and I had sold 115 homes—two short of my goal. However, due to appreciation in the market, my average commission was slightly higher than the previous year and I earned $401,000.

If I had started out the year by saying, *"I want to make $400,000 and I will work hard to do so,"* do you think I would have accomplished my goal? No way! If I did, it would have been pure luck. Do you want your success left up to luck or a well-thought-out plan?

The key to my real-estate action plan was an itemization of daily activities. By tracking my results, I knew where I stood relative to the weekly goal. When behind schedule, I picked up the pace.

The key here is to realize when you are off track before it's too late to change your course.

My Plan for the Blog—*Little Things Matter*

I start every new project with what I call a "brain drain." This is a list of everything I can think of that will go into developing, launching, and implementing the project. After a complete brain drain, I organize my list, set priorities, and assign deadlines to the key elements.

Launching the *Little Things Matter* blog (LittleThingsMatter.com) was no different. My list included major categories such as website design, podcasts, potential profit centers, budget, business formation, social media, an organized list of LITTLE THINGS, and marketing.

Within each category, I listed sub-categories. For example, the social media category incorporated the following activities: learn from and follow experts in the field; join Twitter; get an Avatar; establish my Facebook page; complete my profile in LinkedIn, and learn proper protocol in the social media sector.

Once I was satisfied with the action plan, I reviewed it with the team I had selected for this project. Based upon their suggestions, I refined my plan and began to execute.

The end result: I launched my blog just as I had planned and the results have exceeded my expectations.

LTM Challenge

What's your plan?

Take the concepts I have shared with you and put together a prioritized, daily action plan to achieve the goal that is most important to you. Once you have drained your brain and created your prioritized plan, identify five people who have been successful doing what you plan to do and ask them to review your plan and offer feedback.

Once your final action plan is broken out into daily activities, get started. Be disciplined and be sure to track your results. From time to time, share your progress with your mentors or members of your team and continue to seek their advice.

> **To achieve any important goal, you must first develop a prioritized, daily action plan. Then, using your self-discipline, execute your plan with excellence.**

9. Commitment Gives Power and Purpose

Think of at least one major accomplishment in your life that has made you proud of yourself. Do you have something in mind? Now, think of the initial commitment you made when you started. On a scale of 1-10, how committed were you?

During my career, I have worked alongside thousands of people ranging from Little League ball players to CEOs of billion-dollar companies. One of the things I have learned is that there is a vast difference between simply desiring something and being committed to achieving something.

When you just desire something, you do it only when circumstances permit. When you commit, you accept no excuses, only results.

A commitment is a binding pledge that obligates you to assume a position or carry out a course of action. Making a commitment to what you do— whether in your personal life or your professional life—is one of the most fundamental principles of success.

Commitments are powerful because they influence how you think, how you sound, and how you act. Unlike a half-hearted hope or *best shot*, making a commitment means that you try harder, look for solutions when faced with obstacles, don't look back, and never consider quitting as an option.

Whether it's a relationship or marriage, job or career venture, fitness or health, or a personal improvement goal, the temptation to give up will arise. You must anticipate it and make yourself a promise that the feeling of wanting to quit will not overpower your commitment. Unfortunately most people quit when they feel like quitting, which is why they seldom succeed at anything.

One of the keys to fulfilling your commitments is not to undertake more tasks than your available resources justify. The number of opportunities and decisions we're faced with on a daily basis increases all the time. Given the limits of your time and attention, you'll need to be selective about to whom and to what you commit. It's simply not feasible to do everything you would like. You must decide what is truly important to you and commit only to those things.

LTM Challenge

- Make the decision today that you will never again start a project to which you are not fully committed. Do your research. Know what you are getting into in advance. Consider the obstacles you will face. Then, with your eyes wide open, set your goal, make your commitment, put together your plan, and don't allow excuses to enter your mind.

- Create a Commitment Statement for each of your goals. Take a weight-loss goal as an example. *"I commit to do whatever it takes to lose 10 pounds in 3 months. No matter what obstacles arise and even when I feel like quitting, I will exercise and eat healthy so I can reach my goal."* Write your Commitment Statement on an index card and read it every day.

The only way you will enjoy a long-term relationship with someone is if you are committed to that relationship.
The only way you will enjoy a successful career is if you are committed to it.
The only way you will enjoy life's journey is if you are committed to making the best of it and living life to its fullest.

10. Stretch Your Comfort Zone

People are hardwired to search for comfort; therefore, much of daily life is centered on familiar patterns and habits. While operating in your comfort zone feels good, you are not going to advance your life forward unless you have the courage to push yourself outside your comfort zone.

Think about it. Your comfort zone is where everything feels familiar, safe, and secure, where you know what to expect, and where you are content with the status quo. How can you reach greater heights personally and professionally if you aren't stretching yourself and growing on a regular basis?

Best-selling author Brian Tracy said, *"Move out of your comfort zone. You can only grow if you are willing to feel awkward and uncomfortable when you try something new."*

Denis Waitley, another best-selling author and consultant, has trained numerous U.S. Olympic athletes. He said, *"To achieve your dreams you must break out of your current comfort zone and become comfortable with the unfamiliar and the unknown."*

It's time to get uncomfortable. Let's begin by doing some self-evaluating. Do you avoid doing things you know you should do because they make you feel anxious and awkward, nervous or fearful? What are they?

Contemplate how your life could change if you ventured into the "discomfort zone." Would you feel better about yourself? Would you become more respected by your peers and colleagues? Would you have more self-confidence?

Your first step on the road to greater achievement focuses on the LITTLE THINGS you know you should do but don't feel at ease doing. If you push yourself to do the LITTLE THINGS that thrust you outside your comfort zone, your confidence will begin to grow.

As you build your self-confidence in doing the LITTLE THINGS, you slowly build your confidence to do the bigger things. It works this way for all of us. We start, one step at a time, building our confidence by successfully completing smaller tasks first.

An experience my son Jake had is a perfect illustration. Jake's first job was a bagger at a local grocery store. Jake is an introvert. He is especially shy around strangers. One day I challenged him to start being friendly to the customers whose groceries he bagged. The first day he talked to two customers, the next day five, the next day ten, and by the sixth day he talked to 50 people. Each day Jake told me about his results and I could sense his confidence was growing. One day a head cashier told him he was very good with people—a compliment he thought he would never hear anyone say.

Like Jake, when you first step outside your comfort zone you'll likely feel nervous and perhaps even fearful. But unless you are doing something dangerous or risky, nothing bad is going to happen to you. To the contrary, that knot in your stomach is your signal that growth and opportunity lay ahead.

So feel the fear and do it anyway. Dale Carnegie said,

> *Do the thing you fear to do and keep on doing it ...*
> *that is the quickest and surest way ever yet discovered*
> *to conquer fear.*

LTM Challenge

Identify one of the LITTLE THINGS in this book where your growth has been limited because you have remained in your comfort zone. Start in just one area and as you build confidence in the first one, select a few more LITTLE THINGS where you can break down your barriers and improve. Then fire yourself up and do it without further hesitation!

> **The periods in life when you experience
> the greatest growth and advancement are when you
> do what you have never done,
> go where you have never gone,
> push yourself harder than ever before,
> and do what's uncomfortable.**

11. Our Lives Reflect Our Decisions

One of the most noteworthy and accurate statements of human achievement ever articulated was a statement made by Jim Rohn.

Success comes from making a series of good decisions over time, while failure comes from making a series of bad decisions over time.

After more than ten years of thinking about this statement and watching it play out in the lives of people I know, I am convinced that our lives are indeed a mirror image of our decisions.

Every day we make hundreds of little decisions which I call "Either–Or" decisions. Most of these types of decisions may seem inconsequential at the time, but every decision—no matter how small—leads us closer to or further away from our goals.

Either–Or Decisions

- Do you get up early enough to properly prepare for the day, OR do you sleep in and then rush out the door?

- Do you exercise as you had planned, OR do you blow it off because you don't feel like it?

- Do you make food choices to improve your health, OR do you eat whatever you want?

- Do you pick up the coffee mug sitting on the table, OR do you leave it for someone else to clean up?

- Do you control interruptions to improve productivity, OR do you allow people and things to divert your attention from your responsibilities?

- Do you demonstrate respect by letting people finish their thoughts, OR do you interrupt?

- Do you have a positive attitude even when things don't go your way, OR do you moan and groan?

- Do you genuinely apologize when you are wrong, OR do you water down the apology by making excuses?

- Do you smile and say, *"Good morning,"* to your co-workers, OR do you pass quickly to your desk?

- Do you compliment someone for a job well done, OR do you think they don't need it because they are just doing their job?

- Do you think about what you want to say before speaking, OR do you let the first thing that pops into your head pop out of your mouth?

These little decisions and hundreds of others matter. Your life today is the result of the quality of the choices and decisions you've made up to this very moment. Our decisions determine our physical and mental well-being. Our finances are what they are because of our decisions. Where we work and what we earn are the outcomes of our decisions. The strength of our relationships with friends, siblings, parents, and spouses is directly related to the decisions we have made.

Bottom line: everything we have or don't have and who we are as human beings have been determined by our decisions.

Even though you may choose to avoid accepting responsibility for where you find yourself today, the truth is that you are where you are based on your decisions; there's no one else to blame. You've been in the driver's seat. If you want to change your course, it's time to take control and learn to make different choices and better decisions.

Good Places to Start the Big Change

- Accept responsibility for your decisions and stop blaming others for where you find yourself today.

- Become aware of the decisions you are making every day and start making decisions consistent with the person you want to become.

- Believe in yourself and your ability to make good decisions.

- Start small. Do the LITTLE THINGS right. Make good Either–Or choices.

LTM Challenge

All positive change begins with awareness. If you find your ship in rough seas, turn off your autopilot. Start being aware of all the little decisions you are making. Remember, the outcome of your life will be largely determined by the moment-to-moment decisions you make each day. Don't allow yourself to think something doesn't matter. Everything matters.

> **The hundreds of little decisions you make each day will influence every part of your life.**

12. Making Tough Decisions

In the course of our lives we are faced with many important decisions. Do we leave a secure job with an established company to take a higher paying job with a new start-up company? Should I invest in starting my own business? What home should we buy? Do we relocate to another city? Do I stay in a difficult marriage? How should I invest my savings?

The outcome of any of these decisions will play a vital role in your success and happiness. Make the right decision and life is good. Make the wrong decision and things can get ugly in a hurry.

Ten years ago, I attended a leadership event where a former President of the United States was interviewed. He explained how he makes his most difficult decisions. Of all the decision-making processes I have learned about and implemented, this one is the best.

A President's Process for Decision-making

- **Seek wise counsel.** When he had a critical decision to make, he brought together the highest-ranking, most valued members of his team, including outsiders who had the greatest insight into the situation.

- **Understand the facts.** With this group, the key facts of the situation were clearly outlined so he and everyone on his team would have a complete understanding of the challenge at hand.

- **Discover all options.** On a large board, the team listed every realistic option available to addressing the situation.

- **Reduce the options**. After considering all available options, they narrowed the list down to the best and most obvious choices.

- **Explore the pros and cons of each option.** The team then made a list of the pros and cons of each option. After completing this step, the top two or three top options became clear.

- **Focus on the cons.** They dissected and discussed each con (not the pros). The President wanted to have a plan in advance for how he and his administration would handle each of the potential cons if and when the situation would arise.

- **Make the decision.** After going through this process with his most valued advisors, the President removed all emotions and made his decision based on the facts.

The President was asked, *"Do you look for consensus among the members of your team in making these types of critical decisions?"*

He acknowledged he would always seek consensus among his team. He said, *"If I bring together my best people and go through this process, I would like for us to collectively agree on the best solution."*

Since listening to this interview ten years ago and incorporating the steps outlined, I have made very few bad decisions. This decision-making strategy combined with my life experiences have taught me the importance of seeking wise counsel, to plan for the worst-case scenario, to remove all emotion from the process, and to make decisions based on facts and logic.

LTM Challenge

Good decision-making is similar to learning any new skill—the more you practice, the more proficient you become. While many of your decisions may not require seeking advice of others, at the very least I encourage you to consider all your options and the pros and cons of each. If you will carefully consider the pros and cons of any decision you are making and remove your emotions, you will make better decisions.

> **Your life is a reflection of all your decisions—
> big and small, serious and insignificant,
> short-range and long-range.**

13. The Value of a Mastermind Team

The concept of a mastermind group was first introduced by Napoleon Hill in the 1900s. In his timeless classic, *Think and Grow Rich*, he described the mastermind principle as follows:

> *No two minds ever come together without thereby creating a third, invisible, intangible force which may be likened to a third mind. . . When a group of individual minds are coordinated and function in harmony, the increased energy created through that alliance becomes available to every individual in the group.*

Over the last 20 years I have been honored to serve on boards of multiple companies. Some of my fellow board members were younger than I and some were older. Some were men and some were women. Some represented the United States and some represented other countries. Everyone brought something special and different to the table.

I discovered that what seemed logical to me might not be logical to others, and I learned to respect the differences. The value that comes from bringing together a diverse group of people to discuss ideas, set goals, and make decisions became evident, and I have become a firm believer in the synergistic power inherent in the mastermind principle.

Launching the *Little Things Matter* blog is a perfect example. Here's a glimpse of my mastermind team and the process we implemented.

Step 1. Know the purpose and plan.

> Before forming this team, I put together a document with all my thoughts, ideas, and goals. It was important that I clearly understood and articulated what I wanted to accomplish before involving others in the process. After selecting my team members, I scheduled our first meeting, and put together an agenda.

Step 2. Lay the foundation.

> During the first meeting I reviewed my goals and plan with the team and sought their feedback on each point. This allowed me to gather the views from each person as I walked through the key components of my strategy.

Step 3. Work in harmony.

> In the two subsequent meetings we reviewed the goals and plan for the website design. This included the sample design layouts that my son-in-law Josh gathered. We then reviewed the marketing brief my son Gerrid designed, the identity package my daughter-in-law Jessica created, the Podcast plan my daughter Hannah helped design, and finally the roll-out plan I proposed.

Step 4. Continue consulting the team.

> I continue to confer with my team members on a regular basis, and I am confident that the success of my blog (littlethingsmatter.com) is truly a result of the collaborative effort of my mastermind team.

LTM Challenge

Now it's your turn. The next time you have a project or business concept that could benefit from diverse points of view and experiences, I encourage you to form a mastermind team. The collaborative effort of the team will empower you to make better decisions, expand your horizons, produce a better project, perform above par, and succeed beyond your expectations. While you will seek feedback from the team, remember that you are the leader and you must be the one to run the plays.

> **If you want to improve your decision-making,**
> **you would be wise to put your ego on the shelf**
> **and seek counsel from those you respect.**

14. Get Creative and Think Outside the Box

Do you ever run out of good ideas, or go around in circles trying to come up with a solution for a simple dilemma? I am going to share with you the best technique I know for stretching the mind to come up with new and fresh ideas—from finding a babysitter on New Year's Eve to choosing the right name for a new business venture. Implementing this strategy has forced me to be creative and innovative when it would have been easier to take the standard approach.

Most people probably consider fewer than five possibilities when exploring their options—the ones that immediately come to mind. The problem with this basic approach is that you are limiting yourself by only considering a few familiar choices. If you want to open your mind to a new world of options, you must start to think outside the box.

The next time you need to solve a problem or explore a better way to do something, compile a written list of 20 options—not 5, 10 or 15. Push yourself to come up with 20! The first five things you think of will be the tip of the iceberg. They'll probably be the same five things everyone else would think of in a similar situation because they are the most obvious answers. The key here is to stretch your mind. You will struggle getting up to 13 or 14, but your biggest breakthrough will come when you push yourself to 18, 19, and 20. It is often in those final three ideas where you find the hidden jewels.

Some examples of how you can apply this way of thinking:

- Evaluating where you want to move
- Selecting the location for your next family vacation

- Considering restaurant options for a special occasion

- Contemplating your career options

- Finding ways to cut expenses

- Distinguishing yourself from your competitors

- Looking for new strategies to drive sales

- Providing a higher level of service to your customers

- Choosing different incentive programs for your sales team.

Here's a true story that illustrates the power of creative thinking. A couple's 20th anniversary was approaching and the wife felt like she and her husband had grown apart. Bound and determined to prove her love, she made him an anniversary card listing all the reasons why she loved him. It became quite difficult after #8, but she stuck with it and made it to 20. Reviewing all the reasons she had compiled, she realized she loved him more than she thought! They will celebrate their 34th anniversary this year.

LTM Challenge

The next time you have to solve a problem or think of a better way to accomplish something, sit down with pen and paper and make a list of 20 options. Don't stop at 17. Push yourself to 20.

The intense focus will open up your mind and force you to think of things you normally wouldn't have considered. It won't be easy, but you might just have fun in the process.

Is there anything going on in your life right now where you can apply the strategy outlined in this lesson? If the answer is yes, grab a pad of paper and a pen and get started.

> **To be creative, go where you have never been.**
> **Expand your mind to new ideas,**
> **opportunities, and a fresh way of thinking.**
> **Only then will you discover**
> **a new world of possibilities.**

15. Turn Off the Noise and Think

In today's fast-paced electronic world, the need for quiet time has never been more crucial. The number of interruptions and the resulting stress coming from texts, calls, emails, and social sites has increased. And, of course, we have an endless supply of addictive options at our fingertips to fill our heads with chatter.

If you want to advance your life forward, it's absolutely critical that you block out time to turn off the noise so you can think and process information in silence.

If you want to make sensible life-planning decisions—the kind of decisions that allow you to move ahead in life—you need quiet time to think and process everything going on in your life.

Perhaps it's your desire to build a stronger relationship with your spouse, significant other, or a friend; or that you want to be a more understanding parent. I assume you want to enjoy a successful career and that you want to make enough money to stay out of debt and enjoy the good things life has to offer.

If these things are important, then ask yourself: How much time have I spent in the last month *quietly* thinking about these issues? How can you say something is important, yet not allocate quality time without interruptions to think about it and make thoughtful decisions as to how you can improve that area of your life?

If achieving your goals is really important, then you must make it a priority to block out time and turn off the noise so you can sort out what's going on in your life and make good, course-correcting decisions. Let me offer a few suggestions:

1. **Start your mornings by sitting in silence**. Rather than watching the news, reading the morning paper, or turning on your computer, find a quiet place to sit and contemplate the issues you're facing.

2. **While driving alone, turn off the music and talk shows**. Turn your car into a think tank where you process life and make good decisions.

3. **Go for a daily walk and leave the music at home**. Almost all of my major decisions are made on long walks. Before going on a walk, select a topic you want to think about, and then consider these three questions:

- What's going on? Think about the subject you have selected.
- What are my options? Consider all available options for dealing with the situation.
- What's my plan? Make a decision on what you will do and when.

4. **Block out a period of time and go to a quiet place**. Turn off your phone and thoughtfully review what's going on. Consider all the options available for how you should handle the situation on your mind.

5. **If you have a major decision to make, block out a day.** Get away from your home, and go where you can think in peace and quiet. Consider all aspects of your decisions: pros, cons, risks, rewards, options, and outcomes.

When you make it a priority to block out time in your busy schedule to sit in silence and think about your life and where you are going, you will immediately begin to see the benefit of quiet time.

LTM Challenge

Will you agree to test the principles and strategies outlined by finding 15 minutes today to sit in silence and think about an important decision you need to make?

> **If you want to make life-guiding decisions that will help you achieve the things that are truly important to you, turn off the noise and think.**

16. Accept Responsibility

You alone are in complete control and responsible for the decisions you make and the actions you take; for your success or failure; for your happiness or discontent; for your present circumstances and your future. This bold statement is not intended to frighten or threaten, but rather to empower you.

How we handle responsibility for our decisions and our mistakes is a direct reflection on our character. It's easy to see early on in life who gets it right and who doesn't.

Consider the youth soccer player who always blames the team's loss on the coaches, the officials, and the other players. Or, the young professional with a poor performance record who insists that it's always because of something beyond her control.

At the other end of the spectrum is the group of boys confessing to the neighbor that their baseball put a dent in his car rather than running away, or the husband who humbles himself before his wife and children and apologizes after having lost his temper.

Universally, people who accept responsibility for their actions command greater respect and have a stronger influence. Those who pass the buck or make excuses eventually lose the trust and confidence of others. This is particularly true when that person has assumed a leadership role. No one wants to follow leaders who are unwilling to accept responsibility for their actions.

Here are three actions you can take to accept personal responsibility when something has gone wrong:

- **Reflect**. The first step is to conduct a self-examination to contemplate your action or decision. Before you can make anything right or apologize for a mistake, you must have a clear understanding of where you went wrong.

- **Learn**. When you make a mistake or experience a failure, consider what can be learned. Some of life's most valuable lessons come from the things we have done wrong.

- **Change**. Self-examination and learning by themselves are not enough. If you are serious about accepting personal responsibility and the benefits that come along with it, you must also commit to follow through with change. Continue what's working and change what isn't.

LTM Challenge

From this day forward, will you commit to accepting responsibility for your actions and decisions?

A good place to start is by accepting responsibility in the following areas:

- The circumstances of your life today

- The state of your marriage

- The condition of your financial status

- The quality of your relationships with your children, co-workers, and friends

- The plans for your future

> **Assuming full responsibility for your life**
> **and everything in it**
> **is evidence of your character and**
> **your desire to achieve your personal best.**

17. Your Greatest Obstacle

If I had to identify the single most important factor in personal achievement, it would be discipline—*the ability to do what you know you should do even when you don't feel like doing it.* Discipline—lacking it can be the biggest obstacle between your goals and your accomplishments but having it is the ultimate accelerator of results.

Here's what I mean. I started selling real estate when I was 23 years old. Young and inexperienced, I was at a distinct disadvantage when going head-to-head with experienced and successful Realtors. If given a choice, why would anyone select an immature, unproven Realtor to sell their home?

I knew something had to turn the tide in my favor. Of course, I focused on all the LITTLE THINGS to make a good impression; however, the one thing that turbo-charged my income more than any other single factor was my self-discipline.

Every day I sat in my little cubicle. Struggling to breathe and my heart beating out of my chest, I picked up the phone and made call after call. Pushing myself out of my comfort zone, I kept making calls until I got appointments. By the end of my first full year, I had sold over 60 homes and earned over $250,000. While all the LITTLE THINGS I did played a role in my success, nothing played a larger role than my discipline.

Employing discipline is the most difficult LITTLE THING to do consistently, yet it brings the greatest rewards.

Ten Ways to Develop Discipline

1. **Make a Personal Commitment.** The first step in achieving any goal is to make a commitment to become a disciplined person. This commitment means you will become a do-it-now person and that you will no longer procrastinate doing things you know you should do.

2. **Focus On Your Goals.** Review your goals every morning before you start your day. Pick a quiet place where you can concentrate and visualize. Put yourself in a state of mind where you have achieved your goal and let your imagination go. *You're basking in the satisfaction of a job well done.* What does it look like? What does it feel like? That burning desire that comes from within to achieve your goals will help inspire you to take action.

3. **Do What You Don't Want to Do First.** As you plan your day, block out time to do those things first that require the most

discipline. Whatever it is—prospecting, exercising, or cleaning the house—do it first. You'll be amazed at how the feeling of accomplishment stays with you throughout the day.

4. **Get Enough Rest.** A good night's sleep is essential to maintaining a high energy level. You will sleep better if you avoid eating or drinking before you go to bed.

5. **Eat Right.** Eating right helps to maintain focus and optimize energy levels. Start your day with a breakfast high in protein and low in simple carbohydrates. For lunch, avoid eating foods that make you tired and, above all, don't overeat.

6. **Start Doing the LITTLE THINGS.** Start becoming more disciplined by doing the LITTLE THINGS you know you should do, like making your bed, keeping your car cleaned, taking the garbage out, and picking up after yourself. As you become more disciplined in doing the LITTLE THINGS, you will become more disciplined in doing the big things.

7. **Make the Decision in Advance.** If you are going to tackle an important project in the morning, then don't second-guess your decision in the morning. If you make the decision to exercise every morning at 6:00 A.M., then don't allow yourself to question your decision when you feel like sleeping in. The decision is made; follow through with it!

8. **Make It a Routine.** Set up a routine for doing the things you don't want to do. If you are in sales, set up a routine to prospect for new business every morning from 9:00–11:00 o'clock. If you want to be physically fit, then make exercising a routine.

9. **Get an Accountability Partner.** Do you have a friend, spouse or co-worker who shares a common goal? If so, agree to hold each other accountable in doing what you both need to do.

10. **Reward Yourself.** When you do the things that require discipline, recognize and reward yourself after you are done. If you just finished a big project, dine at your favorite restaurant or do something special to celebrate. If you have been disciplined over an extended period of time, perhaps a weekend getaway would be appropriate.

Consistent discipline in all areas of your life will yield multiple rewards beyond increased productivity. You'll feel more confident and more motivated towards achieving your goals, and you'll feel proud of the person you are becoming. It doesn't get any better than this—feeling that you have done something you didn't want to do but you did it anyway.

LTM Challenge

Over the next several days, be intentional about being more disciplined. If you have neglected to return a call or an email, do it now. If you have a project with an impending deadline, sit at your desk and get it done. If there's something waiting to be done at home, don't procrastinate. From this point forward, use positive self-talk and say, *"If I don't feel like doing it, then I must do it now!"* Then, without further delay, do it.

> **One of the most important keys to success is having the discipline to do what you know you should do, even when you don't feel like doing it.**

18. Measure Your Performance

The advice "measure twice and cut once" is especially useful for carpenters, tailors, and carpet layers to ensure accuracy. However, taking measurements is vital for anyone who wants to improve their performance.

Dr. H. James Harrington—involved in quality and performance improvement projects since the 1950s—tells us why taking measurements is absolutely necessary:

> *Measurement is the first step that leads to control and eventually to improvement. If you can't measure something, you can't understand it. If you can't understand it, you can't control it. If you can't control it, you can't improve it.*

Who Measures?

Any organization, team, or individual who wishes to perform at a higher level or accomplish more must measure their progress.
To clarify, consider if:

- Baseball players never knew their batting average
- Advertisers did not measure the number of people who responded to an ad
- Golfers did not keep track of their scores
- Online shopping sites did not track the conversion rate of website visitors to customers
- Students never knew the results of their tests

- Customer service centers did not measure how long customers were on hold

Without measuring performance, how would they know when they improved?

Why Measure?

The very nature of knowing that something is being monitored causes us to work harder and perform better. There's actually proof of this—it's called the *Hawthorne Effect*. Coined in 1955 by Henry Landsberger, the *Hawthorne Effect* describes a form of reactivity on the part of people whereby they improve an aspect of behavior being measured simply in response to the fact that the measurement is taking place.

Positive things happen when you measure your performance:

- You are able to set goals and evaluate your progress.
- You always know exactly where you stand at any time.
- You can quickly and accurately trouble-shoot your problems.
- You can identify weaknesses to strengthen or skills to refine.
- You are able to see the results of your refinements.

How to Measure

To develop or improve any area of your life, you need to do three things:

1. **Know your starting point**. This is often referred to as your benchmark or baseline—the point from which all progress is measured.

2. **Set a goal**. Noted psychologist Arnold Glasgow said, *"In life, as in football, you won't go far unless you know where the goalposts are."*

3. **Determine how you will measure your progress**. Taking measurements isn't difficult, but it does take time. For example, if you want to save money, carry a small notepad and write down everything thing you buy and the price paid for each item.

You need to develop an action plan. Whether in business, sports, or school, you can't improve what you don't measure. When you track and measure your results each month, you will have new benchmarks that you can strive to improve upon the next month. If you focus on improving your results month after month, you will begin to see amazing changes in your performance and results.

LTM Challenge

Are you ready to get started? Here's a five-step plan.

1. Identify and list the parts of your life that you want to improve. This is a critical component to your success.

2. Document your starting point. As an example, if you want to increase your net worth, subtract your liabilities from your assets and determine your starting point.

3. Set your goals. If you want to double your sales over the next 12 months, write down your target.

4. Determine the key factors that will influence your success. What are the activities that, if done correctly and consistently, will help you achieve your goals?

5. Create a means of measuring your actions and your results. For the concrete measurements like weight, sales targets, and income, use a notebook or software program to record the numbers. With respect to the intangibles, like becoming more personable or developing more discipline, keep a journal to document your progress.

Remember: You can't improve what you don't measure.

As you measure your actions and results, continue to look for ways to make refinements. This is all part of the ongoing process of striving for excellence to be the best at what you do.

> **When you begin to track your results,**
> **the refinements you need to make will be obvious.**

19. What Is Easy to Do Is Easy Not to Do

One of Jim Rohn's most quoted sayings, *"What is easy to do is easy not to do,"* has become a foundational pillar in the *little-things-matter* concept. It has become clear to me that most people know in their gut the simple things they need to do to achieve their personal best; they just don't do them with consistency.

We know we should listen without interrupting, but we still find ourselves interrupting. We know we need to finish our projects on time, yet we find ourselves missing deadlines. We know we should remember someone's name, yet we don't pay attention when introduced. We know we should answer that email or return that phone call, yet we keep putting it off. LITTLE THINGS do matter. In the words of legendary basketball coach John Wooden, *"Little things make big things happen."*

Being consistent in doing the LITTLE THINGS you know you should do has many positive benefits beyond the obvious desired outcome of achieving your goals. You become more respected and admired. You develop new friendships and build deeper relationships. You feel better about the person you are becoming.

So, why don't we do the LITTLE THINGS that are easy to do? The reason is because they are so-o-o-o easy not to do—to neglect, to procrastinate, to promise ourselves that we will do it tomorrow.

Another reason was identified by Napoleon Hill years ago: *"A big success is made up from a great number of little circumstances each of which may seem so small and insignificant most people pass them by as not being worthy of notice."*

What's the reason you aren't consistent in doing the LITTLE THINGS you know you should do? Perhaps you have never focused on the importance of LITTLE THINGS. After all, how much of an impact could letting a few days go by before sending a written thank-you note to a prospective employer? In my mind, a lot—your competitor will get the job!

Or perhaps another inhibiting factor to our productivity comes into play. In a recent interview on a popular blog for aspiring entrepreneurs, I was asked: What was the greatest obstacle you had to overcome in order to achieve your goals? My answer: laziness.

I certainly know the LITTLE THINGS I need to do (I have been making a list of them for over 25 years) and I understand their importance. To this day, though, I have to push myself to do the LITTLE THINGS I know I need to do.

I also want to point out that the habits you exhibit in your professional life are often a reflection of your personal behavior. If your bedroom is a mess, then your car is probably a mess. If you don't have the discipline to clean your home and car, you will likely struggle with having the discipline to do the LITTLE THINGS required of you to achieve your professional goals. You can't be one person at home and a different person at work. You are who you are!

LTM Challenge

If you want to achieve more in your life, if you want to grow as a person and achieve your personal best, then you must become a person who does the LITTLE THINGS that are both easy to do and easy not to do. This will likely be one of the greatest challenges you will ever take on, but if you will make a commitment to use your personal initiative to do the things you know you should do with consistency, your life can be transformed.

> **Your greatest successes in life**
> **come from your disciplined effort**
> **in doing the easy things that are easy not to do.**

20. Build Your Own Brand

What do Coca-Cola™, GEICO™, and Nike™ have in common? They each have a well-developed and recognizable identity or, as they say in the marketing world, a brand. Marketing experts maintain that a company's brand should deliver a clear message, confirm credibility, motivate a buyer to connect, and stimulate loyalty to repurchase.

Just as companies carry a brand, people also carry a brand. Branding is how the world sees you: the impressions you make, the values you stand for, and the qualities that mold your personality. All the LITTLE THINGS you do and say combine to form the foundation upon which relationships are built and maintained.

Chelsea Greenwood—owner of a 1.4 billion-dollar marketing firm—said, *"You are your own brand whether you like it or not. And every experience has a lasting impression."*

Qualities and Actions That Create Brands

How important is the brand we communicate?

- Do you notice people who show evidence of a negative attitude?
- Do you notice people who dress inappropriately?
- Do you notice people who don't seem to be listening? Who interrupt when you are talking? Who talk too much? Who talk too loud? Who use offensive language?
- Do you notice people in restaurants or in line at the grocery store who talk loudly on their cell phones?
- Do you notice people in meetings who keep scanning their phone for messages?

Whether you realize it or not, you form an opinion about people every day. The things they do, the way they look, and the words they speak are branding themselves in your mind. Which co-worker stands out as someone you would rather not work beside? If you were to describe his or her brand, what would it be? Think of your neighbors. Which person is your least favorite and why?

Branding Yourself

Now let's move closer to home. How do you think you have branded yourself? What kind of impressions are you making?

- If your co-workers were to sit in a conference room and describe you, what words would they use?
- If your friends were to chat about your characteristics, what traits or habits would they list?

- If your business acquaintances were to portray you, what picture would they paint?
- If your children were to tell their friends about you, what would they say?
- If your spouse were to "tell all," what characteristics would he or she share?
- At your funeral, as people reflect on who you have been and the experiences they've had with you, what will be their dominant thought? When they listen to your eulogy, what would you like for them to hear?

Tony Jeary, popular author, communication coach, and seminar speaker, warns us about our brands.

> *Every day, in dozens of different ways, you're sending a message out to the world. The wrong message will cost you respect, career promotions, and perhaps relationships. And the right messages will enable you to achieve your personal and professional best.*

Brands Have Power

Who you are—reflected through your brand—will affect many people and many things, such as:

- Your influence with others as a leader
- The level of pay increase you receive
- Whether you are selected for the next promotion
- Whether you are selected to be laid off or retained
- How receptive people are to your ideas

- The type of friends you attract
- How well you are accepted, liked or disliked
- Whether you are asked out on a second date
- What people think about you or say about you
- Whether you are included or excluded in events
- The relationship you have with your spouse or friends
- Your image in the eyes of your children or neighbors
- Whether people want to do business with you
- The level of respect people have for you

Build a brand that consistently makes positive impressions and commands respect. As you adopt the *little-things-matter* way of thinking and improve your brand, the benefits will be noticeable. Your value increases, your relationships improve, and your sphere of influence is broadened. You feel better about the person you are becoming and as your self-confidence grows, you feel like you can conquer anything.

LTM Challenge

Take some time and think about how you want to be viewed by others. Consider making a list of what your brand's defining characteristics will be. When you are clear on the brand you want to build for yourself, start paying close attention to the LITTLE THINGS you do and say. Whether you are greeting a clerk at a convenience store or attending an important business meeting, start presenting yourself to the world in a way that's consistent with the brand you want to create for yourself.

> **The brand you create for yourself is how
> you will be viewed, treated, and remembered.**

21. Increase Your Likability Factor

There are many factors that will influence your ability to foster relationships and advance your career, but likability ranks near the top of the list. Friendly people do the LITTLE THINGS that connect with people and, generally speaking, likable people have greater spheres of influence, get better results, live happier lives, and are more successful. The logic is simple: people are subconsciously drawn to people who are likable.

All the great teachers of personal achievement from Napoleon Hill to Anthony Robbins have talked about the importance of creating a likable personality. Dale Carnegie's famous book *How to Win Friends and Influence People* is one of the best books on the subject, and his teachings live on today. Peter Handel, President and CEO of Dale Carnegie Training, said, *"In order to be the most productive, you must find the right balance of competence and likeability."*

There is no doubt in my mind that being likable can help build a positive brand and increase the value you bring to your family, your community, and to the marketplace.

If your friends, family, team members, or business colleagues were to rank you on the likability scale (1–10) what would they say? Be honest now. How likable are you?

Your Likability Factor Self-test

- When speaking with other people, are you genuinely engaged and interested in what they have to say?

- Does your smile communicate an authentic interest in the other person?

- When people are speaking, are you patient? Do you let them finish before responding?

- Will you get in the back seat of the car so your friend can sit in the front seat?

- Do you accept responsibility when you are wrong?

- Do you show respect for people's time by always being punctual for your appointments?

- Do you avoid complaining when things displease you?

- Do you say *please* when asking people to do something for you, even if they are being paid to do it?

- Do you offer your sincere appreciation to those who have done something to help you, even if it's within their job description?

- Are you friendly in your emails?

- Do you pay compliments to others?

- Do you encourage others when given the opportunity?

- When having dinner at a friend's home, do you pitch in and help do the dishes?

- Do you practice humility—the art of being modest?

- Do you listen more than you talk?

- Do you offer a heartfelt apology, without excuses, when you have offended someone?

- Do you make people feel comfortable when they are around you?

- Do you try to maintain a positive attitude at all times?

How did you do? Are there areas where you need improvement?

Each one of these points represents choices you make. Being likable is about being unselfish and doing the LITTLE THINGS to connect with people and show you care.

LTM Challenge

As you go about your daily routine, start paying attention to the things you do and don't do when communicating and interacting with others in person, online, and over the phone. As you review your daily encounters, look for ways you can increase your likability and become a person who attracts others.

> **When you do the little things to connect with people, your relationships will improve and you will have greater influence at home, at work, and in the community.**

22. The Art of Listening

Being a good listener is one of the most important skills to master if you want to build meaningful relationships or advance your career. When you listen intentionally, you demonstrate your interest in what is being said and your respect for the individual saying it. Thoughtful listening is a magnetic force that draws people to you, building trust and rapport along the way.

Have you ever talked to someone and noticed that he or she wasn't really listening to you? How did it make you feel? Unimportant? Disrespected? Ignored? Remember those feelings and work diligently to ensure that people never feel the same way when conversing with you.

I always value the lessons I learn from my role models. My dad's expertise in this area has been a shining example. He is the best listener I know. Everyone who meets him forms an instant bond with him, and I'm convinced the Number 1 reason for this immediate connection is his heartfelt and sincere interest in others, demonstrated through attentive listening.

Ten Valuable Tips

1. **Make eye contact.** The first step in being an intentional listener is to make eye contact with people while they are talking. Direct eye contact demonstrates genuine interest in the person and the conversation.

2. **Be present.** I must admit that sometimes my wife accuses me of not being present when she is talking, even though I am looking at

her. Perhaps I have that *"The lights are on, but no one is home"* look. When listening, try not to let your mind wander; instead, focus your attention on the person and what's being said. Be aware that people do notice when you are not paying attention.

3. **Don't send signals of your impatience.** When you are listening, don't give any clues that you are ready to respond. Don't point your finger, open your mouth, or fidget. When I see that people are waiting on "pins and needles" to respond, I have a sense they are more concerned with how they are going to respond than with listening to what I have to say.

4. **Don't interrupt.** One of the most prevalent problems in our society is not allowing people to finish a thought without interrupting them. If you start talking at the same time someone else is trying to finish his or her thought, stop and say, *"I'm sorry, please continue."* Then let them finish before responding. Even if what you have to say is important or it's an answer to the question they raised, show them your respect by letting them finish.

5. **Use the two-second rule.** Even though you may feel the urge to present your viewpoint, allowing whatever pops into your head to pop out of your mouth is disrespectful to the speaker. During all of your conversations, wait two seconds after the person stops speaking before you respond. Often people are just pausing to gather their thoughts before continuing the conversation. This is especially important during phone conversations because you can't make eye contact or see facial expressions. If you find yourself talking at the same time someone else is talking, remind yourself to use the two-second rule.

6. **Show a sincere interest.** This is one area where my dad stands out from most people. When he listens he really cares about what is being said, even if it's a subject that doesn't concern him. This is his way of demonstrating that what people say is important and that he values them as individuals.

7. **Listen for the message within the message.** Another one of my dad's skills is to listen for the subtle message hidden in the conversation. Dad says that most people are looking for encouragement, answers, or insights to the subjects they discuss. By listening intently he is able to grasp the topic, allowing him to engage and connect on a deeper level.

8. **Don't change the subject.** When you are engaged in a conversation, don't change the subject unless the discussion is finished. This behavior is obvious in small group settings, business meetings, and social encounters. If you change the subject prematurely, you demonstrate a lack of interest in the discussion and indicate that you think what you have to say is more important.

9. **Respond by asking questions.** Asking questions during a conversation shows a sincere interest in the topic. My dad believes that most people operate at the *feeling* level rather than the *thinking* level. His favorite question is to ask people how they feel about the subject they have raised.

10. **Don't start a side conversation.** When you are part of a group discussion, never start a second conversation with someone near you. Even if the speaker isn't including you when sharing eye

contact with others in the group, don't allow the speaker's lack of courtesy to prevent you from being a good listener.

LTM Challenge

My guess is that, if you are like me, you believe you know the right thing to do and you think you're a decent listener. Can you get better? Will you commit to showing you care about people by incorporating these ten tips into your daily routine? Listening is one of those areas where we can always improve.

> **Being a good listener requires an intentional effort**
> **and a sincere interest in other people.**
> **It is a skill worth mastering.**

23. Make Your Appearance an Asset

First impressions are critical and they happen in a flash or a wink. So Malcolm Gladwell explains in his bestselling book, *Blink.*

> *When you meet someone for the first time, or walk into a house you are thinking of buying, or read the first few sentences of a book, your mind takes about two seconds to jump to a series of conclusions.*

Whether we like it or not, the first impression a person makes is largely dependent on appearance. It's not just a guy being romantic when he says, *"I'll never forget how she looked when I first saw her."* We always notice how people look, what they are wearing, and how they fix their hair.

The first impression you make on people creates a lasting impression. In fact, if you fail to make a positive first impression, you may never be given a second chance. This is especially true when going on a sales call or a job interview.

Companies spend millions of dollars on packaging and branding their products because their research teams have determined that the look and feel of a product impacts buying decisions. Wouldn't it make sense then that we consider how our appearance affects the price we are able to charge for our services?

Author John Malloy first coined the term *Dress for Success* in the 1970s. He asserted that tailoring one's attire, grooming, and overall appearance was important in making a great first impression in a job interview. He also stressed that maintaining a professional look while on the job would aid career advancement.

Your appearance includes everything from the way you groom yourself to the clothing and jewelry you wear. All these little things combine to form your *overall look*. When you find yourself unsure of how to dress, play it safe. It's better to overdress rather than run the risk of being too casual.

As I wrap up the importance of making your appearance an asset, I want to share a personal story that demonstrates the impact our appearance can make. Normally when traveling, I wear jeans and a golf shirt, but on a recent one-day business trip I wore a suit and tie and was feeling good. Arriving at the gate, I greeted the agent by name, smiled, offered a friendly hello, and asked if there were any available seats in the first class section. The agent responded with a smile, upgraded my roundtrip ticket and didn't even charge me. It even seemed that the airport vendors, flight attendants, and other passengers treated me differently, too.

Now this is not to suggest wearing a suit and tie will get you upgraded to first class on airplanes, but it is a reminder that your appearance makes an impression and affects how people view and treat you.

LTM Challenge

One of the fastest shortcuts to success is to learn everything you can from those who are more successful than you, including how they dress. Pay close attention to all the little details: men, the length of the tie, the style of clothing, and appearance of the shoes; women, be concerned with appropriate clothing and jewelry, manicured nails, attractive makeup, and neat coiffure.

> **The quickest and surest way to have others view you as being successful is to look successful.**

24. The Impact of a Smile

If I were to rank all the factors that go into creating a likable personality, I would place a friendly smile near the top of the list. This small act of caring—of acknowledging others—takes little or no effort on our part, yet it has the power to lighten someone's heavy heart. A sincere smile radiates warmth and acceptance. It puts people at ease and makes them feel good. A genuine smile communicates feelings that words alone can't possibly accomplish.

Not only should you smile when you greet people in person, but it's equally important to smile when talking on the phone. Yes, people can actually "hear" your smile. The more you smile in all of your communication and encounters, the more you will naturally draw people to you.

Smiling is contagious. Your smile will lift people's moods and make them want to smile and be happy. My daughter Danielle calls it the ripple effect. Like a pebble tossed into a pond, your smile will spread far beyond the first person that receives it. Danielle's smile brightens up our household whenever she visits. She has earned the coveted family cup with the big, yellow smiley face!

Not only will your smile make people feel welcome, special, and appreciated, but it will also be of advantage to you. You will reap the following benefits:

- Be more likable
- Attract more positive people into your life
- Appear more confident

- Improve your attitude
- Enhance your brand
- Reduce stress and boost your immune system
- Look and feel younger
- Be happier

LTM Challenge

Your smile can be one of the most powerful tools in your personal branding toolbox. For some of you, it will be as easy as lifting your cheeks and showing your teeth; for others, you'll actually need to remind yourself to smile.

I am a happy person, yet smiling has always required an intentional effort on my part. If smiling doesn't come naturally to you, then start focusing on your smile. Put a sticky note next to your phone as a reminder, and start smiling each time you communicate with someone. ☺

> **Smiling is an important step to becoming more likable.**

25. Give a Proper Handshake

Part of the first impression you make is your handshake.

Handshake etiquette, like some of the other lessons in this book, varies depending on nationality and culture. In the United States, the manner in which you extend your hand, the degree of firmness exerted, and the timing of its initiation can set the tone for the relationship.

Let's explore how to give a proper handshake. Perhaps some of you are thinking, *"Come on Todd, I know how to shake someone's hand."* Even so, let's review the basics.

- If you are a male meeting a female, wait for her to extend her hand. If she does not initiate a handshake, do not take it personally or be offended.

- If you are a male meeting another male, always extend your hand first. This is a sign of poise and confidence.

- If you are a female meeting a male, extend your hand first. This will put the man at ease and is also sign of your self-assurance.

- If you are a female meeting another female, be confident and extend your hand first.

These simple rules apply whether you are at a Super Bowl party or a business meeting.

Here are a few more guidelines to follow.

- **When should you shake someone's hand?**

  Every time you greet a male, shake his hand. Every time you meet a female who extends her hand, accept it. This simple rule applies whether it's a formal gathering or a casual meeting.

- **How firmly should you squeeze someone's hand?**

  You don't want to feel like a limp noodle nor do you want to crack their knuckles. My son Gerrid describes it as the "coffee mug" grip—comfortably firm. This is true for both men and women.

  Be considerate when shaking an elderly person's hand. He or she may have arthritis or other conditions that make firm handshakes painful.

  As you shake people's hands make sure you grip their entire hand. If you close your hand prematurely, you will grip just their fingers. I hate it when I do that!

- **When should you let go of your grip?**

  Let go when they let go. I often encounter people who want to hold my hand for an extra few seconds as they greet me. So as long as they want to hold my hand, I hold theirs. Furthermore, you don't want to hurry out of the handshake, as this could be an indication that you are not genuine in your greeting but rather just using the motion as a formality.

- **If you extend your hand to people and they do not extend their hand in return, should you retract your hand or hold it there until they accept it?**

Hold it there until they grasp your hand. Removing your hand conveys a lack of confidence.

LTM Challenge

How would you describe your handshake? Friendly? Firm? Aggressive? Wimpy? If you don't know, shake the hand of a good friend and ask for feedback.

> **Your handshake is more than a greeting.**
> **It's your first opportunity to reveal your confidence,**
> **your genuine interest, and your personality.**
> **Handshakes can speak louder than words.**
> **They really do matter.**

26. Engaging Eye Contact

Eye contact is a form of non-verbal communication that can have profound influence on your social and professional interactions. Here in the United States, eye contact demonstrates interest and respect but whether or not you should look someone in the eye will vary depending on nationality and culture.

Making eye contact is not as simple as it sounds. When is your gaze considered too long? How do you make eye contact when you are speaking with more than one person? If someone doesn't make eye contact with you, what conclusions do you draw about that person?

Speaking With One Person

When you are involved in a conversation with one person, there will be opportunities for you to talk and times for you to listen.

- **When you are talking.** It's acceptable to occasionally look away as you think and collect your thoughts. If there are distractions in the room, make certain to maintain your eye contact with the person who is giving you their attention.

- **When you are listening.** Maintain eye contact with the person talking. Don't stare; rather, meet their eyes in a manner that indicates a sincere interest in what they are saying. If you get a sense that someone is feeling uncomfortable with your eye contact (because they often look down or away during the conversation), occasionally try to break the eye contact for one or two seconds.

This should put the person at ease and make for a more productive conversation.

I vividly recall a painful lesson I learned years ago. After completing a sales training for 200 people, a woman came to the podium, introduced herself, and commented on the presentation. As she was talking, I occasionally looked at the other people waiting to speak with me. She paused, and asked, *"Do you not have an interest in what I am saying?"* Ouch! That one really hurt! Since then I have been conscious about maintaining eye contact with people even when there are distractions that could draw my eyes away from them.

Speaking With Two or More People

When you are taking part in conversation with a group of two or more people, additional challenges are presented.

- **When a member of the group is talking.** You should give this person your full attention by making eye contact. If you don't look at the person talking, he or she will notice. This person will also feel disconnected from you and, perhaps even worse, sense a lack of respect.

- **When you are speaking to the group.** The most challenging part of making eye contact in a group setting takes place when you are the one speaking. When this occurs, your goal should be to share your eye contact equally with everyone in the group. Each person should feel important and included in the conversation.

A recent visit to a car dealership is a perfect illustration of what happens when you don't make equal eye contact in a group setting. My wife had been shopping for a new car and asked me to go with her to look at one she was interested in buying. As the salesman talked to us, he spent 90 percent of his time looking at me and only 10 percent at my wife. When we left the dealership, she told me that she felt disrespected and excluded from the conversation. His lack of eye contact had cost him the sale!

LTM Challenge

Starting today, when you talk with one person, maintain eye contact to show that you believe this person is important and with more than one person, challenge yourself to share eye contact equally with each person in the group. It takes practice but, like anything you practice, repetition will make it more natural.

> **Your eyes send messages. When you establish**
> **and maintain eye contact with people,**
> **you are showing that you have a sincere interest**
> **in them and what they have to say.**

27. Make the Most of Meeting and Greeting

We all know how important it is to make a good first impression when we meet people. Just as a warm smile, a friendly demeanor, direct eye contact, and a firm handshake are important ingredients, so are the words we speak and the interest we show in introductions.

Your greeting is important in all types of situations.

- **When you greet someone who likely forgot your name.** When I greet people I haven't seen for a while, I always take the initiative to introduce myself. *"Hi, Paul. I'm Todd Smith. How are you doing?"* If I don't remember someone's name, I introduce myself by sharing my name and hope they respond by sharing theirs. If people don't offer their name in the greeting, you could say, *"Will you kindly remind me of your name?"*

- **When you are introducing someone to another person.** When you introduce someone to another person, be sure to include each person's name in the introduction.

- **When someone introduces you to another person and does not include your name.** When the person introducing you doesn't include your name, it's likely they forgot it or don't know how to make a proper introduction. In this case, offer a warm greeting to the person you are meeting and be sure to include your first and last name.

- **When you meet someone who doesn't tell you their name.** Simply say, *"I didn't catch your name."* After they respond, repeat their name back, such as *"Bob, it's great meeting you."*

- **When you are not introduced.** I was with a friend in a restaurant recently and a couple of his friends stopped by the table to say hi. He talked to them for a few minutes, but never introduced me. The proper etiquette in this circumstance would have been for him to introduce me to his friends. If others don't introduce you, introduce yourself when the opportunity presents itself. Everyone will feel more comfortable.

- **When you encounter people you don't know.** Have you ever gone to a dinner engagement or meeting, and finding several strangers also in attendance, you stood there awkwardly not knowing what you should do? If appropriate, be proactive and introduce yourself to each person in the room. This makes you stand out from the group as someone with confidence, and puts everyone at ease.

- **When you meet with people you do know.** When you get together with a group of friends or business associates, immediately greet each person with a friendly greeting. As new people join the group, be the first one to show you care by greeting them. My daughter Hannah calls this *"being like a dog."* Dogs are always happy to see people and are the first ones to greet anyone.

- **When you meet with people—some you know; some you don't know.** Always greet the people you know. Don't wait to be introduced to the strangers; take the initiative and introduce yourself to those people. Ask questions to open the conversation and help them feel included.

- **When you greet a receptionist.** Whether you are greeting the receptionist at your dentist's office or at the office of one of your clients, always introduce yourself with a smile and friendly tone. For instance, *"Hi, my name is Dan White. I have a four o'clock appointment with Steve Johnson."* If it's a business appointment, give the receptionist your business card along with your verbal introduction.

LTM Challenge

Following these tips helps you make a positive first impression and enhances your existing relationships. You will be viewed as someone who is friendly and confident, and someone who recognizes the value of making people feel comfortable. Following some of these recommendations may cause you to feel a little awkward at first, but the more you do them, the more comfortable you'll feel.

> **The way you meet and greet people shows them you care about them and tells them a lot about you.**

28. Punctuality Shows Respect

Have you noticed that tardiness is on the rise? People are chronically late for work, for their child's teacher conference or athletic contest, for dinner engagements, even for parties and celebrations.

Tardiness, or lack of punctuality, has been the downfall of many men and women who simply thought it was not important to be on time. Contracts have been lost, friendships have been broken, and reputations have been damaged.

Horace Mann, Father of American Education, felt strongly about this issue. He said, *"Unfaithfulness in the keeping of an appointment is an act of clear dishonesty. You may as well borrow a person's money as his time."*

All successful people view their time as a precious resource. When you are late for appointments with people who value their time, you will have wasted one of their most valuable assets and there's a good chance you'll be viewed as rude, irresponsible, and disrespectful.

Not only should you make every effort to be on time for business-related appointments, but you should also do your utmost to be on time for personal commitments. Valuing your friends' time and earning their respect is an important part of your reputation and your ability to build and maintain relationships.

Whatever your appointment may be—a business meeting, a dinner engagement, or a phone call—you should strive to be on time.

Benefits of Being on Time

- Demonstrates that you are diligent and dependable
- Indicates that you honor your commitments and you can be trusted
- Shows respect for other people's time
- Sets a good example for your children and others who look up to you

Let's look at two scenarios where punctuality is critical.

1. In-person Appointments and Meetings

If you set a goal to arrive at least five minutes early, you'll be more likely to arrive on time, giving yourself a buffer in case you experience an unexpected delay.

There are other benefits as well. Arriving early makes you feel relaxed; you'll be better organized and prepared for the appointment. One more benefit to arriving early means you won't have to make an excuse for being late. I don't know about you, but I hate listening to excuses and, even worse, I hate making excuses.

Throughout my career, I have always strived to arrive for my appointments at least five minutes early to gather my presentation materials and review my notes. Then, at the exact time of the appointment, I rang the bell or entered the meeting location. This was an easy way to make a great first impression.

2. Phone Appointments

When you schedule phone calls, always be clear about who will be responsible for initiating the call. When you don't know who is initiating the call, then accept the responsibility and make the call at the scheduled time.

If you are the person responsible for initiating the call, what kind of impression will you make? Will it be positive or negative? If you call at the exact time of your scheduled appointment, I can assure you, it will be noticed. I have had hundreds of people tell me, *"Wow, you are right on time!"* That comment tells me that I made a memorable impact.

What should you do if your best intentions to be on time fail? Circumstances do arise and it won't always be possible to be on time. If you sense you are going to be late due to stalled traffic or unexpected delays, be respectful. Use your cell phone to call as soon as you know you are going to be late so the person you are to meet with can plan accordingly.

LTM Challenge

Is punctuality a challenge for you?

Let me encourage you to take pride in being a person who is always on time and prepared for your appointments. Set reminders or alarms on your computer or cell phone. Fill your gas tank every time it gets down to one-fourth of a tank so stopping for gas doesn't make you late. Do whatever it takes to be on time.

Nathanael Emmons—a revered American speaker and writer—said, *"I could never think well of a man's intellectual or moral character, if he was habitually unfaithful to his appointments."*

> **When you are on time, you enhance your brand.**
> **When you are late, you devalue your brand.**
> **With intentional effort, you can be punctual**
> **for every appointment.**

29. Using and Remembering Names

Have you ever met someone for the first time who hardly looked you in the eye, said the standard *"Nice to meet you"* greeting without any authenticity behind their words, and then couldn't remember your name five seconds later?

What impression did this person make on you? Would it have required any more time or effort to include your name in the greeting, such as *"It's very nice to meet you, Bob"?* Obviously, the answer is no, but the first impressions created by the two greetings would be as different as night and day.

In Dale Carnegie's timeless book, *How to Win Friends and Influence People*, he discussed the importance of remembering someone's name.

If you want to win friends, make it a point to remember them. If you remember my name, you pay me a subtle compliment; you indicate that I have made an impression on you. Remember my name and you add to my feeling of importance.

Many of us believe that we are horrible at names and reinforce this belief by telling people, *"I just can't remember names."* Our brains record the fact that people's names are not important and forgetting someone's name becomes a reality.

With concentrated effort you can break that habit. First, determine for yourself that remembering someone's name is a LITTLE THING that matters—it's a pleasant sound in his or her ear and it says, *"You are important."*

Second, when you greet people, whether it's the first or the tenth time, make it a point to say their names in your initial conversation. For example, *"It's a pleasure to meet you, Sharon."* And then when the conversation concludes, use her name again. *"Sharon, it was a real pleasure getting to know you."*

Be careful that you don't overuse someone's name. If it's said too often, people could question your authenticity.

Six Ways to Help You Remember Names

Remembering someone's name is a difficult skill to master, but if you make it a priority, you will stand out from the crowd in your social and business relationships. Here are six tips for remembering people's names:

1. **Pay attention when you are introduced**. Focus on them, not on yourself. Listen to information about who they are and what they do.

2. **Ask to have the name repeated**. If you don't hear the name clearly or understand the pronunciation of someone's name, kindly ask the person to repeat it. If you still don't understand, ask how to spell it and then try to say it. People with hard-to-pronounce names are accustomed to having their names mispronounced and appreciate those who show an interest in getting it right.

3. **Create a strong mental picture of this person**. What makes this person unique? Notice the facial features and the body build. Repeat the person's name to yourself several times as you note these distinguishing characteristics.

4. **Use an association.** You could also associate the name with an object or their occupation that will remind you of their name when you meet later. Sometimes I try to think of someone else with the same name and then make the connection between the two people.

5. **Write it down**. Carry a notebook with you when attending group events and jot down a person's name with an identifier, like Steve, the guy with red hair; or Sue, the computer programmer from Boston. When on the phone, write down their names and use them appropriately.

6. **Ask for business cards in a business setting**. Seeing the name in print will help you remember it. Making notes on the back of the card helps jog your memory.

LTM Challenge

Start to be intentional about remembering people's names. Begin by eliminating "what's-her-name" and "what's-his-face" from your vocabulary. Use all the tips I have outlined, starting with the easiest one—repeat the person's name at both the beginning and the end of the conversation. You will soon become a respected and appreciated person who remembers people's names.

> **Remembering someone's name is one of the**
> **LITTLE THINGS that makes a favorable impression.**
> **Whether it's in a social or business environment,**
> **it's a valuable asset, building instant rapport**
> **with new people you meet.**

30. Build a Strong Online Reputation

A significant component to your overall brand (how the world sees you—your character, habits, speech, choices and decisions) is your online presence.

In today's highly networked and technological world, you can be assured that every potential employer or business partner, prospective client, or college admissions officer will search the Internet to learn as much as they can about you. It's even likely that someone will "check you out" before asking you for a date. What they find influences their opinion and can either close doors or open up new opportunities.

Ten Ways to Enhance Your Online Brand

1. **Create a personal website.** You can control what people find when searching your name, or you can leave it up to the search engines. If you don't currently have one, I suggest creating a simple one-page website. In 1999, I made the decision to take control of my online brand when I set up mine at toddsmith.net. You can register your name for a small fee and use a free template to create your website.

2. **Join Facebook.** According to Facebook's own statistics (facebook.com), the social networking site has more than 500 million active users, of which 50 percent logon in any given day. Facebook offers more opportunities for networking and building relationships than any other website. If you want to promote a business, blog, or non-profit organization, you can also create an *Official Page* in addition to your individual profile. Facebook is a powerful way to connect with people and enhance your online brand, if you use it wisely.

3. **Create a LinkedIn profile.** More than 75 million professionals in over 200 countries use LinkedIn (linkedin.com) to make connections and exchange information, ideas, and opportunities. If you are a professional who does not have a LinkedIn profile, you run the risk of appearing out of touch.

4. **Consider Twitter.** Depending on your line of work, you may want to consider opening a Twitter account (twitter.com). Take a look at what your competitors are doing on this social networking site to determine if it makes sense for you to tweet.

5. **Complete your profiles.** When you set up an account with any social media or professional networking site, take the time to complete your profile. Having an incomplete profile will likely make a negative impression. Even worse, you are missing an opportunity to market yourself.

6. **Select appropriate photos.** Every photo you post on a website, including your Facebook profile picture, is how the world will see you. Make sure all photos accurately depict how you want to brand yourself. Unless you want to be seen as someone who parties all the time, get rid of the photos that paint you in that light.

7. **Use discretion when promoting your business.** If you own your own business and want to promote it using social media, learn the proper protocol first. Let me also strongly discourage you from promoting any business through your personal Facebook page.

8. **Think before you write.** We generally don't need to be reminded to think before we speak but, far too often, I find that people don't think before they write. Be conscious of the words you use when you post or make a comment on websites, blogs, or forums. Avoid using inappropriate language, texting language, or slang. Since every item of information on the Internet is archived or cached, anything you post today has the potential to be seen by others ten years from now.

9. **Evaluate groups and fan pages.** Keep in mind that the groups you join or the social media sites on which you become a fan tell the world what's important to you. In most cases, even if I am not a friend or connected with people, I can still see which groups they follow.

10. **Google™ yourself.** As you create your personal brand on a variety of sites, networks, and other platforms, your name will begin to pop up on search engines and social networks. Google yourself and determine if the chatter is positive or negative. Consider setting up a Google Alert for your name that can help you monitor your brand. Using Google Alert, you will be notified when your name appears on a website or blog.

LTM Challenge

I strongly suggest that you evaluate your online brand. Take 30 minutes and study the websites and social networking sites where you already have a presence. Consider what kind of impression you are creating. Are your profiles complete? Where else could you or your business be visible? Above all, if you are going to have a presence on any website, demonstrate pride in who you are and how you are portrayed.

> **Your personal and professional success
> is greatly influenced by the impressions
> you make on others—both online and offline.**

31. Attending Special Dinner Engagements

LITTLE THINGS matter in every area of our lives, including what we say and how we act when attending social events. While I'm far from being the male version of Miss Manners or Emily Post, I have learned how to handle myself at important dinner engagements as I traveled the world meeting with valued clients, prospective partners, and business colleagues.

20 Tips for Making a Positive Impression at Dinner

1. **Prepare in advance.** Make sure you know what you are going to wear (including accessories) and give yourself plenty of time to get ready. I learned this lesson when I left my tuxedo shirt at home and didn't realize it until I was getting dressed in my hotel room.

2. **Look your best.** Discover what the dress code is in advance and make sure you look your best. When unsure, you are better off overdressing than underdressing. You only get one chance to make a first impression.

3. **Be on time.** Arriving on time shows your respect to the host or hostess and other dinner guests.

4. **Greet everyone.** Greet each dinner guest with a warm smile and a firm handshake. If appropriate, repeat his or her name such as, *"It's nice meeting you, Dan."*

5. **Wait to be seated.** Allow the host or hostess to direct the seating arrangements.

6. **Don't be the first to order an alcoholic drink.** Water is a good first choice. If other guests order an alcoholic beverage, you can order one as well.

7. **Go with the flow.** If everyone at the table is drinking plain water, don't ask for sparkling water. Keep requests simple, especially if you are at someone's home.

8. **Focus your attention on the person talking.** When someone is talking, maintain eye contact with this person. This demonstrates your respect for the person and indicates that you are interested in the topic.

9. **Include everyone when talking.** When you are talking, share eye contact with each person at the table to include them in the conversation and make them feel valued.

10. **Think before you speak.** Don't be quick to jump into the conversation. Instead, be a respectful listener and observer. When you do talk, carefully consider what you say.

11. **Don't talk about yourself.** Resist the temptation to talk about yourself unless asked. Show an interest in others by asking questions. Listen attentively and continue the conversation accordingly.

12. **Don't start a side conversation.** Be sure to focus your attention on the person speaking, even if they aren't making eye contact with you.

13. **Don't change the conversation.** Unless a conversation is clearly over, don't change the topic being discussed. This could be perceived as a lack of interest in the current subject or even boredom.

14. **Excuse yourself at the appropriate time.** Wait until there is a pause or a shift in the conversation if you feel it's necessary to leave the table. Otherwise, your exit will be a distraction and the person speaking could feel you don't value what is being said.

15. **Wait until everyone is served.** Wait until everyone has received his or her food before you start eating.

16. **Don't cut up all the food on your plate**. Good table manners dictate that you cut up your food as you eat, rather than to cut it all up at once.

17. **Don't drink too much.** Of all times you don't want to over drink, important dinner engagements rank at the top of the list.

18. **Pass it.** If someone asks for the rolls that are in front of you, pass the basket without taking one. If you want one, after they help themselves, you can ask that it be passed back to you.

19. **Be on your best behavior.** Sit up straight; leave your elbows off the table; don't pick your teeth, and remember all the other things your mother taught you!

20. **Help clean up.** If the dinner engagement is at someone's home, offer to help clean up. Simply ask, *"Would you please allow me to help you?"* When they accept your offer, help clean up until the job is finished or until your host or hostess wants to take a break. If they decline your help because they would rather continue the conversation in another room, ask them again when the party is over.

Emily Post leaves us with a final word:

> *Manners are a sensitive awareness of the feelings of others. If you have that awareness, you have good manners, no matter what fork you use.*

LTM Challenge

Let me encourage you to follow these tips at your next dinner engagement. If you are intentional about incorporating these into your behavior, you will make a positive impression on everyone in the room and you'll feel good about yourself and the person you are becoming.

> **Practicing good manners is an easy way
> to enhance your image and influence.**

32. Accept Compliments Graciously

From a very young age, we were taught how to accept a gift: say *"Thank you"* and something nice about the gift. Never say you don't like it (even if you don't) or you will hurt the feelings of the giver. This advice, as good today as it was when you were five years old, applies whenever you receive a gift—and that includes the gift of a compliment.

Graciously accepting a compliment in any setting is not only good manners, it's a sign that you are confident and self-assured. It's an effective way to build rapport. Properly accepting compliments is one of those LITTLE THINGS that can enhance your reputation.

There are a number of theories as to why people have a hard time accepting compliments including such diverse things as wanting to appear modest, not feeling as if the compliment is deserved, or doubting the sincerity of the person giving the compliment. What you may not realize, however, is that rejecting, deflecting, or not properly acknowledging a compliment creates a negative impression. It discounts the intentions of the person giving the compliment, sends a message that you think their opinion is off base, or suggests that you doubt the value of your own abilities or characteristics.

Given the world we live in with so many people being self-absorbed, it's becoming rare to receive compliments. So when someone takes notice of something we've done well or how we look and makes an effort to tell us, we owe it to the person to acknowledge his or her thoughtfulness.

Compliments come in many forms and there is a proper way to acknowledge praise, commendation, or admiration.

- **Make eye contact**. Look the person in the eye when you respond to communicate sincerity and self-confidence.

- **Say *"Thank you."*** A sincere, unhurried *"Thank you,"* along with a smile and eye contact is often enough.

- **Don't explain anything.** If you feel inclined, you can follow your "thank you" with something positive. Doing so communicates desirable character traits such as friendliness and positivity. If you can't keep it brief, are tempted to explain or rationalize your action or accomplishment, leave it at a simple *"Thank you."*

LTM Challenge

During the next week, listen for compliments given to others. Make a mental note about how many times you hear people rejecting or ignoring compliments they receive.

Give more compliments than you normally would. Notice how people respond to you. Put today's advice into practice the very next time you receive a compliment.

> Acknowledging a compliment paid is a simple
> yet effective way to express your appreciation,
> make a positive impression,
> and build a favorable reputation.

33. Leave a Positive Last Impression

Making a good first impression is an important component of your brand, but equally important is your last impression. When you leave a relationship, an organization, or a place of employment, the last impression you create is how you will be remembered. And how you are remembered will likely have long standing implications.

A positive first impression may have landed you a job, but a negative last impression could jeopardize your chances of getting one in the future. People who leave a place of employment with an honorable attitude (when it would be tempting to do otherwise) stand out as people worthy of respect.

This trite but appropriate saying is true: *What goes around comes around.* One damaged relationship can have far-reaching implications. If you leave a relationship on unfavorable terms or you handle yourself in a tasteless manner, there is no upside. No matter how you try to justify your actions, you will likely regret your behavior for months and years to come.

When you are wronged, disrespected, or mistreated in any way, how you react is your choice. You are in control. You can act irresponsibly and seek revenge, or you can handle yourself in a mature manner responding with discretion and dignity.

The benefits of leaving on pleasant terms are evident.

- **You gain respect.** If you handle yourself with class—no matter what the circumstances are concerning your departure—people's respect for you grows.

- **Your reputation is protected.** It is very difficult to speak negatively about people who handle themselves in an honorable and admirable fashion.

- **Your self-image increases.** When you handle yourself properly and you do what you know is right, your self-image is enhanced and you have peace. This is especially true if doing the right thing is difficult.

- **You receive favorable references.** You'll most likely need references from your employer and co-workers to secure a new job. It's not uncommon for a prospective employer to Google™ you or to speak personally with your former co-workers before taking the interview process to the next stage. If you want to advance your career and build your market value then your track record will be just as it sounds—your track record.

LTM Challenge

Life rarely proceeds exactly as we plan it. There will always be situations where you have to make a change. Sometimes changes are momentous, like a marriage or a career; others not quite as serious. Regardless, be proud of the way you leave a situation and make your last impression a good one.

> **The first impression you make determines
> how people view you;
> the last impression determines
> how they remember you.**

34. Develop Unquestionable Integrity

How important is integrity? I have included it in my list of LITTLE THINGS, but it is also a very big thing. Integrity is a character trait that goes by many names: truthfulness, honor, reliability, honesty, veracity, genuineness, or authenticity.

President Dwight D. Eisenhower, World War II General and 34th President of the United States, spoke of integrity:

> *The supreme quality for a leader is unquestionably integrity. Without it, no real success is possible . . .*
> *If a man's associates find him guilty of being phony, if they find that he lacks forthright integrity, he will fail. His teachings and actions must square with each other. The first great need, therefore, is integrity and high purpose.*

If you want to achieve long-term success in the business world, you must absolutely be a person of integrity. Sure, people can get to the top without integrity, but all we need to do is turn on the news or read our local paper to see they don't stay at the top. Those people who lack integrity are eventually exposed and, when they are, their world comes tumbling down.

Author Tom Stanley's research reported in his book, *The Millionaire Next Door*, and the sequel, *The Millionaire Mind*, demonstrates that first generation deca-millionaires (those with a minimum net worth of ten million dollars) statistically had 38 behaviors or traits in common. The Number 1 value was integrity. Their vendors, friends, and even their fierce competitors commented that these mega-achievers had *"fanatical levels of integrity."*

Integrity is equally important in our personal relationships. It is the foundation upon which all long-term friendships and marriages are built. Nothing will destroy a friendship or a marriage faster than a lack of trust. When people have given me cause to question their integrity, I can forgive them; I can even love them; but it's painfully hard to ever trust them again. How about you? When people have been deceptive, misleading, or have cheated or lied to you, do you still trust them? Trust is one of those rare qualities that when it's lost, it's almost impossible to regain.

LTM Challenge

After reading this lesson I hope it goes without saying: Don't ever—even once, for any reason—do something that could cause people to question your integrity. No matter what it is, it isn't worth the long-term consequences. Few things spread faster than the fact that someone can't be trusted. The best way to keep people from doubting your integrity is to never give them a reason to question it.

> **There is no character trait more important in achieving long-term personal or professional success than integrity.**

35. Uncover the Truth Within

A large facet of our moral character is honesty. Telling lies to others to gain power or money will eventually defeat us, but equally damaging are the lies we tell ourselves.

Clouded views, poor judgments, and a negative self-image are the by-products of this self-deception and, unless you start being honest with yourself, it's highly unlikely you'll ever be a success at anything.

When you are honest with yourself, you see things exactly as they are. There's no smoke and mirrors, no pretending or playing games, no justifying or making excuses, and no denying the facts. It's just the cold, hard truth.

The other day I had a craving for a couple of slices of pizza. In my car on the way to the local hole-in-the-wall Italian restaurant, I knew I was going to eat one of the unhealthiest foods I could put in my body. I didn't try to justify my decision by saying the cheese is healthy because it comes from cow's milk; the crust, because it comes from whole grains. The sauce is healthy because it comes from tomatoes; the sausage, because it contains protein. I didn't play games with myself. I knew I was making a poor food choice. Period.

But we're not just talking about eating pizza when we know it's bad for us. It's about making a conscious effort to see all things as they are. Lying to ourselves may make a bad situation seem better in the short term, but in the long term it can only make things worse.

Here's an honesty checklist. How do you respond to these questions? Your first response will reveal the true answer.

1. Do you think you are overweight? If three doctors were to give you an exam, what would they say?

2. Do you eat healthy foods? If three nutritionists were to look at your dietary intake, would they agree?

3. Do you have the tendency to drink too much alcohol? What would your family members say?

4. Do you listen to people without interrupting? What would the last five people you talked to say?

5. Do you tend to overreact in stressful situations? What would your co-workers say?

6. Are you in control of your life, or is your life in control of you? Think about it. You know the truth.

How did you do?

When you are truthful, it helps you develop a keen sense for what's right and wrong. You'll see things more accurately. You'll make better decisions. By truthfully evaluating your faults and weaknesses, you'll be more open to the process of change.

Because I was honest with myself over the years, it allowed me to refine my craft. By accurately viewing my performance with a critical eye, I found areas where I could improve. The ongoing refining of our skills, talents, and personal characteristics is key to achieving our true potential.

LTM Challenge

Being honest with yourself is a sign of maturity—a sign that says you are willing to take a good look in the mirror of truth. I want to encourage you to start being truthful with yourself all the time, in every situation. While it may be painful at times, it's part of the process we all go through if we want to improve our lives.

> **The day you start being 100 percent honest**
> **with yourself is the day**
> **you will start making better decisions.**

36. Build Trust With Confidentiality

In this lesson you will learn the immense value of keeping things confidential that are intended (directly or implied) to be private.

One of the most important interpersonal elements in any relationship is trust. Once trust is established, respect generally follows, deepening friendships and solidifying business relationships. In business, trustworthy people are more likely to sell more products, build a larger customer base, receive more raises, and enjoy earlier promotions.

One of the most common, telltale signs of someone who cannot be trusted with confidential information is the person who says, *"So-and-so told me this in confidence, but I know you won't say anything."*

While it might feel good to get the inside scoop, think about the person whose information they promised not to divulge. How do you think this person would feel about their private information being disclosed? Personally, I would think twice about sharing my own sensitive information with this person.

Being a person of integrity who can be trusted with private information goes beyond not sharing information you were asked to keep in confidence. It also includes what's called implied confidentiality. This is when you use discretion not to pass on information others wouldn't want shared.

To gauge your trustworthiness in this area, ask yourself how likely you would be to share any of the following:

1. You are on a business trip and having some drinks after hours. A colleague overindulges and ends up passing out in the lobby after a series of pretty funny antics. Do you share this story back at the office?

2. Your friend is going through a difficult period and tells you about some of his or her personal challenges. Do you discuss what your friend told you when meeting with another friend?

3. You and your spouse had a real blowout. Do you vent to your friends?

Each of these situations involves implied confidentiality. Even though the colleague, the friend, and the spouse don't specifically ask to keep their actions or information private, discretion dictates that these types of things ought not to be broadcasted. I'm sure you would agree that there's quite a bit at stake for the person at the center of each situation. Careers, reputations, and relationships could be irreparably damaged.

Guidelines for Keeping Confidences

- Never share information that you have been asked to keep confidential.

- Use good judgment when it comes to matters of implied confidentiality.

- Keep things confidential that were intended to be confidential even when a relationship breaks down. It's a small world.

- Do not vent your private marital or relationship issues with your friends.

- Politely decline when someone wants to let you in on someone else's secret.

LTM Challenge

Are you willing to make a commitment to never again divulge anything that should be kept confidential? It's not an easy commitment, but recognize that your decision to share or not to share will affect whether people trust you.

As in most matters, there are exceptions to every rule, and that is true here, too. Don't take the oath of secrecy so far when someone's health or well-being is at risk.

> **Maintaining confidentiality builds trust
> in all our valued relationships.**

37. Your Word Is Your Bond

There's an old adage that you probably heard from your parents: *You're only as good as your word.* Translated it means: *You do what you said you would do when you said you would do it.* But do you? It's ironic that although almost everyone will admit to placing a high value on keeping their word, fewer and fewer people actually follow through.

Keeping your word (demonstrating that you can be trusted) plays a powerful role in how you are viewed by others. It is the foundation of your personal character and your brand. In the long term, it strongly influences how you view yourself. And, quite frankly, it dictates whether you are a person who is respected and accepted or ignored, disregarded, and scorned.

Honoring your word is integral to a good marriage, solid friendships, and mutually rewarding business relationships. It also includes carrying out the LITTLE THINGS you say you will do—such as calling when you said you would, remembering to let your neighbor's pet in as you promised, turning in the report on time, or showing up to the party after sending in your R.S.V.P.

If you become known as someone who doesn't honor your word —even occasionally—the repercussions can be devastating. Once respect is lost, it is often impossible to regain. Backing out of a commitment usually results in guilt and time wasted in an attempt to avoid those we've let down. When we've shirked a commitment, it often takes more time and emotional energy to circumvent a situation or repair a damaged relationship than it does to keep our word.

Undoubtedly there have been and will continue to be times when you agree to do something that you later regret. However, once you have agreed to do something, don't back out or procrastinate. Don't hope the other party will forget or wait for them to remind you. When you have given your word—implied or directly—that you will do something, you must do it and do it when it is expected.

After you have fulfilled your obligation (however painful), learn from the experience. Why was it so hard to follow through? Was it a matter of time? Did you not consider what was involved? Whatever the reason, figure it out and know that it should factor into your decision-making process the next time you are asked to do something similar.

Living up to your commitments also contributes greatly to your self-image. Whether you realize it or not, falling back on your promises is a sure way to erode your self-esteem. The more frequent the occurrences, the more risk there is of a sustained negative self-image. Think of the last commitment you failed to fulfill. How did this experience make you feel about yourself?

Becoming a person of your word boils down to a couple of basics.

- **Think before you commit.** With few exceptions, there's no reason to act hastily. It's perfectly acceptable to tell someone that you need time to think about the request. Take an hour, an evening, or a day to think it through. Consider all that is involved and decide whether or not it's something to which you are willing to commit your time and energy. If not, politely decline.

- **Once committed, don't back out.** I have asked myself hundreds of times: What was I thinking when I made that commitment? Even so, I mustered everything to uphold my end of the bargain. Honoring my word is essential to who I am; it's one of my core values. As a result, I am very careful with the commitments I make.

LTM Challenge

- Starting today, become the person who lives up to your word and does what you say you will do, even when circumstances change.
- Uphold your word with a good attitude. Remember that it was you who said yes in the first place.
- Take every opportunity to learn from your commitments so that you can make better decisions in the future.
- Do you have any unfulfilled commitments? Do them now. You will feel better.

> **If your quest is to be the best, strive to be known as a person who always does what you say you will do when you say you will do it.**

38. Speak Well of Others

At some point, you have no doubt experienced what it feels like to have people talk behind your back and you know how painful it can be.

Speaking ill of others reflects poorly on our character. Not only do unfavorable words hurt the other person, they also damage our credibility and reputation in the process. When we judge or criticize another person, others often perceive our comments as a ploy for our own personal gain. When our words persuade others to our point of view as to the faults and shortcomings of someone who is not present, we are taking unfair advantage of that person. This holds true whether we're talking about an individual, a group, or a business.

A recent trip to my local supermarket is a good example. I only needed a bag of ice so I took a shortcut through one of the empty lanes to get to the service desk. A cashier happened to be in that lane and said he could help me. I told him I didn't realize his lane was open because he was standing off to the side. He proceeded to tell me about the *stupid policies* of the store, ranting the entire time and spoke nothing but ill of his employer.

While he was unloading his personal dissatisfaction, I was questioning his motives and forming my impression of him. I immediately sized him up as an inconsiderate employee who failed to see himself as a store representative with an obligation to act and speak accordingly.

Where your attention goes, so goes your emotional energy. Focus on positive things and your life will be positive; focus on negative things and your life will be negative. When you say destructive things about others, it has a detrimental effect on your emotional energy and your attitude.

On the other hand, when you brand yourself as someone who refrains from speaking disapprovingly of others, people's respect for you grows. When you refuse to say something negative about someone, you demonstrate self-control and concern for others.

In the words of Dale Carnegie, *"Any fool can criticize, condemn, and complain but it takes character and self-control to be understanding and forgiving."*

Do not, however, confuse speaking of someone in a derogatory way with participating in a formal critique, such as job performance reviews or when you are asked to point out deficiencies for the purpose of helping someone improve in certain areas. In these instances, use tact and diplomacy to focus on performance issues and always avoid personal attacks.

LTM Challenge

I encourage you to follow these tips to avoid conversations that could damage your reputation and the reputation of someone else.

- Refuse to engage in negative conversations about others.

- Decline to be part of groups who speak poorly of others. If you are surrounded with people who thrive on criticizing others or talking behind their backs, it may be time for you to reconsider with whom you spend your time.

- Avoid making unflattering comments about other people as your comments influence people's views of you. Sometimes figuratively (and sometimes literally) I bite my tongue when I am on the verge of saying something negative. I do so knowing that quelling the urge to speak my mind on impulse helps me show consideration for others, uphold my values, and maintain my reputation.

> **You can build a reputation that commands respect by refusing to speak negatively of others in all circumstances—regardless of who is or isn't present.**

39. There Are Two Sides to Every Story

Beginning in the days of World War II and for decades after, famed radio broadcaster Paul Harvey shared *The Rest of the Story* with millions of Americans. After presenting news stories, he surprised listeners each time with a true twist at the very end and concluded with his signature sign off, *"And now you know... the rest of the story."*

Although Paul Harvey died in 2009, I can't help but think of his influence on the idea that there are always two sides to every story and that it's to our benefit to make sure we know and understand both sides before making a judgment or rendering an opinion. You may not agree with what's being said, but it's wise to know all the facts before you speak or act.

Whether it's your best friend complaining about his or her spouse, a co-worker annoyed with another employee, or a newspaper columnist writing a political story, bear in mind that there's always more than one perspective to a story. Not everyone sees, experiences, and recalls things in the same way.

I think most people can relate to the "Uh-oh" feeling that comes right after learning we've made a fool of ourselves for having argued a point, only to find out that we didn't have all the facts and made an error in judgment. This is sometimes followed by a tactful retreat or as they say, *eating of our words*. We all may do it on occasion, but repeated rushes to judgment could damage our reputation and jeopardize our relationships.

LTM Challenge

It's natural to be influenced when we hear or read something—especially if it's well presented—but you may not have the whole story. It's not necessary to weigh in on every issue. When you reserve your strongly held beliefs for the things that really matter, your opinions will carry more weight and your point of view will command greater respect.

From this point forward, make sure you have all the data on which to base your judgments. When addressing a conflict or challenge, be sure to reserve your opinion until you have heard both sides of the story.

> **Every mountain has two sides;**
> **you don't know what is on the other side**
> **until you have crossed over the summit and**
> **witnessed the view yourself.**

40. The Damaging Effect of Complaining

Psychologists say that people generally complain for one of two reasons—as a way of enlisting people to agree with their point of view or as a means of making conversation since negative observations often yield a bigger response than positive comments. Sadly, that's true, but neither of these reasons outweighs the fact that no one likes being around people who are chronic complainers.

Whining is a childish trait and can be a difficult habit to break once it has become a part of your communication style. Nevertheless, breaking the habit of complaining is essential if you wish to be viewed as someone whose words carry weight and whose opinions matter.

Some forms of complaints are obvious, but other forms are often disguised as commentary or critique. They may appear more subtle but are just as damaging to your reputation.

When you do have a *legitimate* complaint to communicate, you can do so in a productive manner by following these guidelines.

- **Have a purpose.** Having an objective for complaining means that you wish to accomplish something that is both reasonable and specific. Complaints without purpose include things like: the way your favorite NFL team played on Sunday, the weather, or the traffic on the Interstate. These things may bother you to a degree, but you can't do anything about any of them, so why spend your time complaining about them?

- **Offer a proposed solution.** Whenever you complain, be prepared to offer a reasonable solution.

- **Be understanding.** People are not perfect and most employees are doing the best they can. It's also important to recognize that what may be logical to you may not be logical to someone else. Make a point to accept and value the differences in people. Recognize that we all come from different backgrounds and have different life experiences. Have a little more patience; be a little more forgiving.

- **Treat others with respect and kindness.** If you must complain in certain situations, such as being served cold food in a restaurant, discovering a billing error, or challenging a warranty discrepancy, describe your situation in a way that shows respect to the individual listening to your complaint. Oftentimes, these people are not the ones at fault. They just answered the phone or waited on your table. And even if it is their fault, there's no need to speak to them in a disrespectful manner.

LTM Challenge

The good news is that breaking the habit of complaining is something you can do all on your own. Here are a few suggestions to get you started.

- For the next 24 hours, make an effort to catch yourself each time you complain—at home, at work, and out in the community. Being aware of your tone and how much you verbalize your dissatisfaction with other people or things is the first step toward ridding yourself of this bad habit.

- Listen to the people around you, especially out in public. Notice how they speak to servers, customer service representatives, and other workers. What does this tell you about them? What does the way you speak to people in public say about you?

- The next time you find it necessary to lodge a legitimate complaint, make sure it meets the criteria discussed—purposeful, solution-oriented, understanding, kind, and *whine-free*.

> **Complaining is harmful to your reputation.**
> **If you must criticize, make sure your words are constructive**
> **and that you handle yourself in a way that**
> **reflects positively on your character.**

41. Earn Respect by Practicing Humility

Comedian Rodney Dangerfield complained about it. Parents demand it. Professional athletes expect it. Respect—everybody wants it, but not everybody gets it. Respect is not a gift; it is something you must earn. Take the professional athlete as an example. We might admire him for his skill, or envy his million-dollar salary, but we respect the athlete for the effort and attitude he exhibits on the field or court or during an interview.

What is the attitude that quickly wins respect? Humility! An attitude of humility is one of the most significant predictors of someone who is revered. Humble people have a modest view of their own importance. In order to adopt the habits and behavior patterns of humility, it's important to recognize its evil nemesis—arrogance. Very few things damage one's reputation quicker than arrogance.

Just as people can sense if someone has a good or bad attitude, they can also sense if someone has an arrogant attitude. An arrogant attitude is often communicated by one's bragging, but it's also revealed by how one treats other people. Arrogant people are prima donnas (vain people who find it difficult to work as part of a team), often pushing others aside, believing they are the only ones qualified to get things done the right way. When working on teams, they come across as overbearing and egotistical and they are quick to dismiss the ideas and contributions of others.

By contrast, a humble leader allows others on the team or at the table to express their views. This spirit of humility allows leaders to expand their options when working on a project by drawing on new ideas of the people with whom they are working.

One of the challenges for most high achievers is finding the right balance between communicating with confidence and humility. This can be tough—especially for entrepreneurs and sales people whose livelihood depends on marketing themselves and relying on their accomplishments to obtain future business. We want to appear as confident in ourselves and in the services we offer, but we don't want to cross the line so that we appear prideful.

To help understand these qualities, let's look at the definitions of confidence and humility.

- Confidence is having a self-assurance arising from an appreciation of one's strengths and abilities.

- Humility is having a modest opinion of one's own importance or rank.

There's no reason why these two character traits can't coexist. In fact, when they do, it's hard to find a more powerful combination. The key is to do so without coming across as egotistical.

Here are a few tips to communicate what I call "quiet confidence."

- Let your prior record, actions, and associates speak for you. Avoid what would sound like boasting about yourself or your accomplishments.

- Limit the times you speak freely about yourself and your achievements. Acceptable times are those occasions when you are communicating the value you bring to a personal or business relationship.

- Consider how you can communicate your message in a way that does not sound like bragging.

- If you will be giving a presentation to a group of people, tell the person introducing you the highpoints of your accomplishments that you feel people should know. It is always better for others to speak of your achievements, than for you to do it.

By its very nature, humility is not an attitude we ever perfect. It's a lifelong endeavor that requires constant monitoring, especially since arrogance—egotism, superiority, and conceit—is always tugging at our human nature.

LTM Challenge

Start being aware of what you say when talking about yourself. Limit the times you speak about yourself and your accomplishments to those times when you are selling yourself. When you do need to "sell yourself" or your services, remember to communicate your message in a way that remains focused on your client or customer and what you can do for them.

If you are in a leadership position, make sure your team members can sense your appreciation for them and their contributions. Don't ever forget that humility is an attitude and everyone can sense who has it and who doesn't.

> **One of the admirable traits among high achievers
> is humility—that rare quality of being
> modest and respectful.**

42. It's a Small World

As they waited to be called into the courtroom, two teachers were discussing their jury duty assignments. Juror #1 mentioned how glad he was that he was able to get a substitute and didn't have to ask the assistant principal to stand in. Juror #2 complained, *"The assistant principal at my school couldn't run my class if she wanted to!"*

Juror #1 asked, *"Where do you teach?"* Juror #2 responded and said, *"Lakeview High School."* Juror #1 replied, *"You must be talking about Elaine. She's my wife."*

What an awkward situation! Like Juror #2, too few people realize that what they say and do can offend people and will likely have a ripple effect on their lives, lasting perhaps a week or even a lifetime.

At the heart of this lesson is the reality that, indeed, ours is a small world, made even smaller by the Internet. Whether you are an employee, sales professional, or entrepreneur in today's world, there is a good chance people may already have searched your name online to see what they could learn about you.

Career advocates warn us not to burn bridges or ever say anything negative about a former employer in an interview. I would go a step further and recommend that you never burn bridges in any area of your life or speak negatively about anyone—period!

Some people have carelessly burned bridges behind them, offensively and unpleasantly ending a relationship. In many cases, they may have passed the point of no return.

Consider these very plausible situations:

- The woman at the athletic club whom you have treated with a cold shoulder may be the wife of your husband's most important customer.

- The man standing behind you in the grocery store who heard you being disrespectful to the cashier may be one of the business leaders on the scholarship committee at your daughter's school.

On the other hand:

- The elderly person whose tire you changed on the side of the road may be the brother of the chairman of the board at your company.

- The hostess at your favorite restaurant whom you always treat respectfully may be the daughter of your most valued prospective client.

The older I get, the more of these small-world *coincidences* I see. I have come to understand and appreciate that we live in a connected world and these connections play a vital role in our lives.

Benjamin Franklin said, *"It takes many good deeds to build a good reputation, and only one bad one to lose it."* You never know whether an offended person might enter your life again at a future date. Why risk alienating anyone?

Every interaction you have with someone does one of two things: it helps your reputation or it hurts it.

LTM Challenge

It's time for a reputation checkup.

Your reputation is a lifelong accumulation of your actions and your interactions with the people around you. What does your reputation say about you today? What would your previous neighbors, co-workers, or business acquaintances say about you if they were asked for a personal recommendation?

Have you burned bridges in your past? Most of us have at one time or another, but it is possible—and advisable—to make amends. Oftentimes, when you go out of your way to restore a previously damaged relationship, you make a stronger, more favorable impression than if you were to ignore the issue.

> **Build a reputation that speaks for you
> when you are not around.**

43. Attitude Is a Choice

Winston Churchill, one of the greatest influencers of attitude in the 20th Century, said, *"Attitude is a little thing that makes a big difference."*

Your attitude is a powerful mindset, affecting every part of your life—career, relationships, self-image, and even your health. Defined as a person's feeling or emotion toward a fact or situation, attitude is a person's mental outlook, one's temperament, mood, or viewpoint.

We tend to think there are only two kinds of attitudes, positive and negative, but truly there are many. Friendly or reserved, confident or insecure, cheerful or depressing, compassionate or callous, determined or indecisive, peaceful or destructive, appreciative or ungrateful are just a few examples. Aren't these all attitudes that are reflected through the tone of your voice, the expression on your face, your body language, and how you relate to and treat others?

Attitude is a key component in defining one's personality. Your attitude affects how people see you—whether they like or dislike you, whether they want to be around you or avoid you, how they respond to you, and whether you gain or lose influence with them.

Think of someone you know who always seems to have a good attitude. Is this someone you enjoy being around? Is this someone you would hire? Is this someone you would buy something from?

Now think about someone who always seems to have a bad attitude. Is this someone you enjoy being around? Does this person give you energy or draw energy from you? If you were having a party, would you invite this person? How likely would you be to embrace any idea that comes out of his or her mouth?

Your attitude is a choice, and that choice is completely within your control. Just know that your choice will make a big difference. The benefits of positive thinking and positive attitudes are well documented. Researchers have found that people with positive attitudes are happier, healthier, and live longer than those with negative attitudes. Do you need any more reasons to do what it takes for you to control your attitude?

LTM Challenge

Expect things to get better. Look at your life with optimism and hope. When you expect things to go well, you will see opportunities you would otherwise miss. When you expect things to turn out poorly, you wouldn't see an opportunity if it hit you in the face.

Obviously, there will be times in your life when it's very hard to have a positive attitude, but don't ever forget that YOU are the one in the driver's seat, and your emotions will go where you take them. Start paying attention to your attitude and keep it positive!

> **Positive people have greater self-esteem,
> greater inner power and strength,
> and command more respect.**

44. Choose to Be Happy

Although it may be tempting to dismiss a call to happiness during troubled economic times, world strife, or personal grief as overly optimistic or too simplistic, I believe these are just the occasions for a reminder that when it comes to happiness, all of us have a choice. In fact, choosing to be happy is one of the few essential decisions that we get to make regardless of age, stage of life, or present situation. It's a decision that can't be taken away, and no one else can make it for us.

Each one of us gets to choose, every single moment of every day, whether or not we want to be happy. It's the same as choosing which dress or tie to wear, or choosing to eat pancakes and syrup instead of bran cereal. Just as you choose the outfit because it makes you look good, you choose the pancakes to satisfy your sweet tooth craving. You choose to be happy because it's how you want to experience life.

Happy people are more likable and desirable to be around. Isn't it amazing how we're drawn to people with sunny dispositions? One of the consequences of this phenomenon of human nature is that happy people regularly benefit from the enthusiastic help and cooperation of others.

Researchers have determined that happy people have stronger immune systems, endure pain better than unhappy people, and live longer. They have greater and longer opportunities to enjoy life and everything in it.

Happiness leads to greater job productivity that often results in higher income. So why not choose to be happy?

No doubt, you can think of many reasons. You're not where you want to be in your career; you've experienced financial setbacks; your children aren't living up to your expectations; your boss doesn't appreciate your efforts; your neighbors aren't friendly. And your list goes on. Let me suggest that these are not *reasons* at all. They are *excuses* for not being happy.

Dale Carnegie explains it this way: *"Happiness doesn't depend on any external conditions; it is governed by our mental attitude."* You alone are in control of your attitude and making the decisions to improve your life. Choose to be happy and then take the necessary steps to make it so.

I can personally attest to the connection between happiness and an improved quality of life. Many years ago, I decided that I would be intentional about choosing to be happy. I didn't just say I wanted to be happy; I found out what I needed to do to make happiness a daily reality for me. Though I'm fortunate that I have experienced a rewarding career and professional life, it's not my achievements that are to be credited for my happiness and the quality of life I now enjoy. Rather, it's the little decisions I consistently make each day that continue to help me in my choice to be happy.

LTM Challenge

If you've never considered happiness as a choice before today, there has never been a better time than right now to choose happiness. Take control of your emotions and start focusing on the good things in your life and the person you want to become. As you do, you will begin to feel the happiness in your life.

> **Choose to be happy.**
> **It's an attitude that will improve every part of your life.**

45. Learn to Enjoy What You Don't Enjoy

Everything in life is not fun. Everything in life is not interesting. We are always faced with things that we have to do even though we don't want to do them. It might be paying bills, working on a project with uncooperative co-workers, prospecting for new business, cleaning the house, or attending a social event with your spouse. The question is this: Do you take on these tasks with a good or a bad attitude?

I see and talk to people almost every day who are clearly doing things they don't enjoy. Next time you are out, observe the teller at the bank, the checkout person at the grocery store, or the guy repairing something at your house. Do they appear to be happy doing what they are doing, or are they distinctly telegraphing their displeasure? How can you tell the difference? Notice their body language. Watch the expressions on their faces. Listen to the tone of their voices and the vocabulary they use.

The other day I was at a restaurant and the server was clearly having a bad day. Her unpleasant attitude was apparent in the way we were greeted, by the snarl on her face when she took our order, and by the unkind way she interacted with other servers.

Let's take a look at the two options that were available to the server to determine which one makes more sense.

Option #1. She could have a bad attitude, take our order, bring us our food, get a bad tip and feel worse.

Option #2. She could control her negative feelings, take our order, bring us our food, get a good tip and feel better.

Regardless of her choice, she was going to have to take our order and bring us our food. Whatever was bothering her wasn't going to go away with her downbeat disposition, nor were dollars going to start falling from the sky to brighten her day. There was no upside to be gained from having a bad attitude.

Here is one of my life's philosophies: Whatever you have to do—do it with an upbeat attitude. If it's something that you don't enjoy doing, and you don't have the opportunity to change it, find a way to do it with a pleasant attitude.

Tips to Enjoying the Things You Don't Enjoy

- **Think positively.** If you consistently say to yourself that you don't like to do something, you won't. Your brain will register this attitude and remind you of it the next time you are in a similar situation. Guard your thoughts and make sure you don't allow them to become negative. Be creative and challenge yourself to look for the good in the things you don't enjoy.

- **Learn from the experience.** If you think positively, there's a good chance something can be learned from the very thing you thought you didn't enjoy. Even if the only thing you learn is that you can do things you don't like with a good attitude, you will have learned one of life's most valuable lessons.

- **Focus on the benefits**. When you make the decision to enjoy the things you don't enjoy, you will be happier. You'll feel better about yourself, and people's respect for you will grow. Always keep in mind there is NO benefit that comes from doing things with a bad attitude.

LTM Challenge

Take a few minutes today to identify the things you don't enjoy doing. Be candid with yourself. Do you think others can sense you don't enjoy doing them? How might your attitude be affecting people's view of you?

If you are going to do something, find a way to enjoy doing it. If you sense a bad attitude is starting to brew, remind yourself that you are in control and the choice you make affects you and everyone around you.

> For every unpleasant situation you face,
> it's your choice how you respond.
> You can choose to make the best of it
> or let it get the best of you.

46. Be Positive During Difficult Times

To encourage determination in the face of challenge, I have often quoted the inspirational words of Joseph P. Kennedy (father of U. S. President John F. Kennedy) *"When the going gets tough, the tough get going."* The determination I am referring to is your resolve to maintain a positive attitude during difficult times.

Bad things happen to all of us. It's a given. We may not have been dealt the cards we would have liked; nevertheless, we have a choice to make. Do we wallow in self-pity, play the victim role, fold and go home? Or do we make the best of it and muster the strength to continue to play?

I cannot imagine one positive thing that comes from having a dejected attitude during challenging times. Can you? Even if you were laid off from your job, lost a loved one, encountered a serious health challenge, or were denied a well-deserved promotion, what good would come from having a negative attitude?

The truth is that a negative attitude actually compounds your problems.

Handling adversity with a positive attitude is especially important if you are in a leadership position. When times get tough, people always look for leadership. The people who step up their game and lead with a positive attitude during troubled times will always earn the respect and admiration of those who look up to them.

This is another one of the LITTLE THINGS that's easier said than done, so let me suggest some specific strategies to help you have a positive attitude during trying times.

- No matter how bad things get, if you hold your head high, you will always find joy and beauty around the corner. As long as you don't fixate on the negatives, the positives will reveal themselves to you like a shining star in the dark sky. Concentrate on all that is good in your life and remember that your attitude is a choice.

- Look at your challenges as opportunities to grow and develop yourself. If you lost your job, it may be time to reinvent yourself and find one that better utilizes your value to the market. If you lost a big sale to one of your competitors, determine what went wrong and make changes so you win the next time. It's through disappointments that we learn life's most valuable lessons.

- You can get through any difficult situation as long as you keep moving in a positive direction. Sometimes you will feel like you're trudging through quicksand, but as long as you don't stop, you will eventually make it. Remember, spring follows winter and the light of day follows the darkness of night.

People who muster the strength to look for the positives in the face of difficulties are worthy of respect by peers, friends, and team members. Lead by example and set a positive tone for all your interactions.

LTM Challenge

The next time you get down, hear bad news, or are faced with a difficult challenge, remember that how you respond is your choice.

> **Challenging circumstances are a part of life.**
> **Whether they get you down or make you stronger is your choice.**

47. Manage Discouragement

It's true—we all get discouraged from time to time. It's just one of those potholes we hit on the road of life. Even though you may have everything you've ever wanted, you're still going to face times of deep discouragement.

When we get depressed, our attitude and emotions turn negative. When this happens, our productivity takes a nosedive, and we tend to withdraw from others. Whatever the goal is we're working toward, the risk of giving up runs very high.

Since it can have such a negative impact on every area of our lives, learning to deal with disappointments and the temporary discouragement that may result is an important part of managing our lives.

Most of the time when I find myself feeling down, it's because I am tired, had a rough day, or someone said something that is bothering me. If I just get a good night's rest, I usually awaken with renewed energy and an improved outlook.

Sometimes, however, I need more than just a night of rest. I need to explore the root cause of my discouragement so that I can understand it and respond accordingly. I'd like to share my five-step process for learning about and properly dealing with discouragement.

1. **Ask yourself why you are discouraged.** Take a few minutes to sit down in a quiet place and make a list of reasons why you're feeling this way. Keep in mind that you can't control something you don't understand.

2. **Probe further.** Once you are clear on why you are discouraged, explore deeper to understand what's causing you to feel this way.

   - Is it because of unmet expectations? If so, make sure your expectations are realistic and that you are not setting yourself up for failure.

   - Is it because you have let yourself down? If so, what are the specifics of the situation?

3. **Look at the bigger picture**. After you have gained a perspective on the issue that is the source of discouragement, try to understand your relationship to it by asking yourself these questions:

   - Am I feeling this way because I am burned out? Do I need a break?

   - What part of this situation is my fault? What can I do differently?

   - Am I making progress, but just slower than I had hoped? What lessons have I learned? Am I a better person because of this experience?

   - Should I go to someone I trust and respect for some insight and perspective on this matter? This is always a big help to me because much of my discouragement stems from unfulfilled expectations. Often a fresh perspective is all I need.

4. **What's the plan?** Next to each item on your list, write down your plan to address the issue that is bothering you. Don't accept a long-term sentence of discouragement. Nothing puts an end to discouragement like productive mental and physical activity.

As I reflect on all the times I have felt dejected, I realize that these were times when I needed to grow. Perhaps I needed to learn to set better expectations; maybe I needed to be more careful in whom I placed my trust; or possibly it was time for a new perspective.

5. **Count your blessings.** If necessary, make a list of all the things for which you are grateful. Often, we focus on the one thing that's wrong and overlook the 99 things that are right. When you make a conscious effort to write down what's going well in your life, it sheds a new light on your situation.

LTM Challenge

Vincent van Gogh, the famous Dutch painter, said, *"In spite of everything I shall rise again: I will take up my pencil, which I have forsaken in my great discouragement, and I will go on with my drawing."*

Will you pick up your pencil, overcome your discouragement, and persevere?

> **Learning how to process and manage discouragement leads to a happier and more satisfying life.**

48. Don't Worry About What You Can't Control

If you are like most people you probably spend more time worrying than you should. Worrying about job security, project deadlines, health, shrinking budgets, rising taxes, the housing market, world poverty, our children's safety, even the weather. Some things we can control, others we clearly cannot. The key to maintaining a positive attitude in life is to know the difference.

I heard years ago that 92 percent of the things people worry about are beyond their control.

If you are troubled about something you can control, like whether you are going to lose your job, then step up your game. Come in early, stay late, offer to work on a weekend, or volunteer to take on additional responsibilities; do anything you can think of to increase your value. If you end up losing your job, you can bet you'll get a better reference.

If you are concerned about your health, exercise regularly, eat a well-balanced diet, and refrain from smoking.

On the other hand, if you find yourself worrying about something like the safety of your son or daughter serving in the military, whether the government is going to raise taxes, or whether the coming storm will deluge you with rain, understand that there's no action you can take to make any impact on these events or circumstances. You cannot control these things; worrying about them will just cause stress and affect your overall attitude. In the long term, worrying about what you can't control puts your health, happiness, and longevity at risk.

LTM Challenge

Make a list of the things you worry about. Divide that list into two categories:

1. Concerns you can do something about
2. Concerns beyond your control

Beside each of the items you can control, include an action item. For instance, if you worry about the ten pounds you've recently gained, put together a plan to do something about it. If you're concerned about an impending deadline, make a list of all the things required to get the project completed.

Make a commitment to attack everything within your control and be intentional about not worrying about the things you can't. At first, you'll find it hard not to worry about the things you can't control, but if you use self-discipline and refuse to worry about them, it will become easier.

> **One of the traits of positive people is that they don't worry about things they can't control.**

49. Avoid the Toilet Bowl Syndrome

For years I have been teaching sales people and entrepreneurs about what I call the "toilet bowl syndrome." Here's how it works. When you get down for whatever reason, your sales usually follow. When your sales drop and your income takes a dive, you get even more depressed. Day after day, the vicious cycle continues. The only way to stop this downward spiral is to take action. You have to rip yourself out of the ditch of sorrow and self-pity and take control of your thoughts and emotions.

It doesn't take much to see that the toilet bowl syndrome has universal applicability. Allowing yourself to emotionally get down affects every part of your life. It's almost impossible to focus on advancing your career. Your home life and relationships suffer because no one enjoys being around people who are an emotional drain. Even your health is at risk.

I realize this is one of those subjects that is tough to face. You probably want to turn the page right now and read something more positive. Don't!

Facing the facts and becoming aware of the effect of repeated negative thinking is the first step you need to take to bring about change. Next, you have to take control of your emotions and be in command of your thoughts. Easier said than done, I know. But you must accept the fact that you alone are in control of your thoughts and your life—not circumstances, not chance, not fate. If you don't change your thinking, how can your life improve? If you don't climb out of that whirlpool of despair, how can you succeed?

Reversing the spiral of negative thinking will be difficult initially. It's as if you are fighting a strong current in the ocean. But the sooner you get started, the better off you'll be. You'll make progress, one stroke at a time.

If you are struggling with negative thoughts and emotions, let me help you turn the tide.

Five Ways to Stop the Downward Spiral

1. **Learn from your disappointments** and then move on so you can begin the process of achieving your goals.

2. **Focus on your blessings** and you'll begin to see positive things occur. Small improvements will increase your happiness and new doors of opportunity will open as you begin to attract like-minded people into your life.

3. **Read** *The Power of Positive Thinking* by Dr. Norman Vincent Peale. Many years ago, I listened to the audio version and it has had a profound impact on my thinking and overall attitude.

4. **Control your internal dialog**. Make sure the conversations you have with yourself are positive and constructive. Remember, where your attention goes, so goes your emotional energy.

5. **Internalize the sage advice of Jim Rohn,** *"Disgust and resolve are two of the great emotions that lead to change."*

When you get down, you have to be the one to pull yourself out of your funk or you may find your life swirling like the water in the toilet bowl—downward. Don't feel sorry for yourself and hope that someone is going to come along and help you out of your doldrums. This decision is up to you. It's your life.

LTM Challenge

Let me encourage you to take responsibility for your thoughts and emotions and begin running your life rather than letting your negative emotions run you. Let this be the day when you step up to the plate and say, *"Enough is enough; I am going to take steps to stop the vicious cycle of negativity in my life."*

> **You are in control of your emotions and thoughts;**
> **therefore you are the ONLY person**
> **who can change them.**

50. Be Grateful for What You Have

Part of enjoying life's journey is learning to enjoy what you have while pursuing what you want. This is not easy when you feel like life has thrown you a series of curve balls. During these times when you are feeling down and discouraged, stop and think about all the things for which you can be thankful.

Perhaps your life may not be turning out *exactly* as you envisioned it would, but if you can see, you have it better than the 40 million people worldwide who are blind.

When you are crying in the shower about a problem, be happy you are standing in a shower. Over one billion people don't have this ordinary convenience.

Next time you want to complain about your job, just remember there are 239 million adults who wished they had a job to complain about.

No matter how bad you think your life is, stop to consider that you have it better than more than 775 million illiterate people who wouldn't be able to read this book even if it was written in their native language.

Charles Dickens said, *"Reflect upon your present blessings, of which everyone has many; not on your past misfortunes of which all people have some."*

If you will focus on the things you are truly blessed to have, rather than your problems and what you don't have, happiness won't seem so elusive. This change in attitude will improve everything: your career, your relationships, and your self-esteem. It's almost impossible to advance your life forward when you are preoccupied with problems and have a negative outlook on life.

LTM Challenge

Regardless of whether you think your "life is like a bowl of cherries" or it seems like you've been run over by a locomotive, take ten minutes today and make a list of everything for which you are thankful. Save this list and when you find yourself feeling discouraged, re-read it. Get ready to appreciate the magnitude of your own abundance.

> **No matter how bad you think your life is,**
> **there are millions of people around the world**
> **that would switch with you in a heartbeat.**

51. Play the Odds to Win

One of life's greatest lessons came to me fairly early in my career. I would often get feedback about the things I said or did that caused offense or people found objectionable. My first reaction was, *"If you don't like it, tough! I can't make everyone happy."*

But with age came maturity and I began to think differently. Sporting an arrogant I-don't-care-what-you-think attitude certainly wasn't going to take me where I wanted to go. It was then that I learned about playing the odds. Playing the odds involves making decisions that give you the greatest probability of success. Does the reward justify the risk?

We always have choices. When faced with a choice, play the odds to win. Ask yourself whether your actions or words could cause a problem or are likely to turn someone off. And if so, find an alternative. One of the best ways to increase your odds is to seek feedback and criticism, sometimes even before you take action.

Let me give you three examples:

1. While the use of profanity is on the rise, there is a large majority of people who are offended by foul language, including the use of God's name in vain. If by using inappropriate language you run the risk of turning people off, tainting your reputation, losing a friendship or a career advancement, why do it? Is there an upside? Could it be that people like to hear you swear and as a result of your profanity, their respect for you will grow? I doubt it.

2. I'm sure you've heard this rule: No politics and no religion at the dinner table. Parents wisely know the danger of discussing these two topics in a social setting for they can cause an escalation of emotions like the rising mercury in a thermometer on a hot day. Unless you absolutely know the political leanings or religious views of a person, it's best not to discuss these issues that may cause anxiety and offense. You could be running the risk of alienating a friendship or a professional relationship.

3. Recently, I received an email from a young entrepreneur who started his first company. He indicated that one aspect of his personality was to use humor and sarcasm but that, in his leadership position, some people found his comments inappropriate. He asked if he should be his authentic self or if he should change. My response included one question and one statement. The question, *"Who do you need to be as a person to achieve your professional goals?"* and the statement, *"You need to decide what's more important, your offensive humor or your professional success."*

Think about all the decisions you make in any given week. There are no doubt hundreds where you must consider this question: Is my doing this or saying that worth the risk of turning someone off? You always have a choice.

LTM Challenge

I want to encourage you to be thoughtful of what you are doing and saying, and avoid anything that people might find offensive. It's just not worth the risk.

Play the odds and increase your probability of achieving your goals. Life is hard enough already. Make decisions that give you the greatest chance of being a person worthy of respect. In every situation, you can choose the option that won't have an adverse effect on your personal reputation.

> **If you want to win in the game of life,**
> **make decisions that**
> **put the odds in your favor.**

52. Set Realistic Expectations

Expectations—we all have them from a very early age, yet many of us don't learn how to set and manage them until well into adulthood.

From the child whose birthday wishes are never quite fulfilled, to the spouse who always feels as if he or she is the one who's giving more, to the manager whose team never seems to get it quite right—the expectations we set for ourselves and those around us have the power to influence our success and satisfaction in life.

As you progress through this lesson, ask yourself this question: Are my expectations helping or hurting me?

Because expectations have such far-reaching, powerful consequences in every area of your life, I want to share some of the best advice I've learned when it comes to setting proper expectations for yourself, those around you, and those you lead.

When we set false or unrealistic expectations, we put ourselves at risk for a host of unwanted outcomes ranging from perpetual frustration and disillusionment to damaged relationships. Even worse, the negative experiences of unmet expectations are a serious drain on our motivation and often lead to negative thinking. Some examples to illustrate this point:

- *"If he won't do more in this relationship, why should I?"*
- *"If Joe isn't making calls, why should I?"*
- *"It doesn't matter what I do. Things are never going to change."*

On the other hand, the benefits of learning to set proper expectations are well worth pursuing. People who master the art of setting proper expectations generally have a happier outlook on life, experience fewer disappointments, and less discouragement.

You can begin to set appropriate and realistic expectations when you recognize that there are three main categories of expectations.

1. **Expectations for yourself.** You know what you are capable of, but it's wise to be cautious about setting expectations for yourself that are unrealistic. There is a fine line between pushing yourself to do better and setting yourself up for failure. Find that line so you don't limit your own accomplishments or, at the other end of the spectrum, become depressed and unfulfilled. One effective way of finding the right balance is to keep in mind that change is incremental; it doesn't happen overnight, no matter how much you want it.

As you explore the right increment for your personal growth, never lower your expectations to a level where you are no longer challenged. The day you stop challenging yourself to become a better person is the day you begin falling back in life.

2. **Expectations for family, friends, and colleagues.** Whether or not you are conscious of it, you have set expectations for those around you. In personal relationships, take care when considering what you expect of others. Because every person is unique, no two people see things exactly the same way. Therefore, it's simply not realistic to expect that people—even those closest to you—always know what's in your heart and mind and are actively working toward meeting your expectations.

   When you start counting on others to meet your unspoken needs and desires, you set yourself up for heartache and disappointment. Make sure your expectations are sensible and appropriate to the relationship. To be fair and to avoid disappointment, do your best to consistently communicate those reasonable expectations.

3. **Expectations for those you lead.** In a management position, you should set expectations for your team, but it's critical they know, understand, and agree to the expectations you set for them. Expecting those you lead to fulfill expectations you have not clearly communicated is a sure-fire recipe for disappointment and dysfunction.

LTM Challenge

How about performing an expectation checkup to determine if the expectations you are setting are appropriate? If you find yourself constantly disappointed in yourself and in others, you are likely setting expectations that are unrealistic or too high. Here are a few checkpoints to get you started.

- Are your expectations realistic and aligned with your goals? You should always strive for improvement, but make sure it's incremental and achievable.

- How are your current expectations affecting your relationships with your spouse, friends, and co-workers? Don't make a list of the things they should be doing to make you happy. Instead, make a list of the things you can do to make them happy. You'll be amazed at the difference in your personal level of satisfaction.

- Know that your expectations are not the same as everyone else's. That's normal! If you're in a leadership position, don't set expectations that have not been clearly communicated, no matter how basic they may be. Basketball coaching legend John Wooden started every season teaching his players how to put on their socks to avoid getting blisters!

> **If you set realistic expectations for yourself**
> **and those around you,**
> **you'll avoid many of life's blisters**
> **and enjoy happier, more fulfilling relationships.**

53. Invest in Your Relationships

One of the most important keys to living a happy, healthy, and fulfilling life is your ability to build and maintain meaningful relationships. There is solid, scientific evidence that having friends can extend life. People with abundant social support develop stronger immune systems and are less likely to suffer from depression, anxiety, and the physiological effects of stress. Harmonious relationships with friends and family members are the fabric of our lives—the glue that binds, bringing us joy and meaning.

If you want to build a long-term relationship—one that feeds and sustains you in the different areas of your life—be deliberate about the time and attention you give it. Contributing your time, energy, and effort into growing your relationships begins with a fundamental, universal truth: What you give, you get back.

- When you show love, you receive love.
- When you show respect, you earn respect.
- When you smile at people, they smile back at you.
- When you show an interest in others, they become interested in you.
- When you are friendly to others, they are friendly to you.
- When you encourage others, they encourage you.
- When you do things for others, they do things for you.

I like the way Anthony Robbins explains this concept.

> *Some of the biggest challenges in relationships come from the fact that most people enter a relationship in*

order to get something. They're trying to find someone who's going to make them feel good. In reality, the only way a relationship will last is if you see your relationship as a place that you go to give, and not a place that you go to take.

If you want a relationship to last over a long period of time, you must offer value and meet the needs of the other person. It's a lot like a savings account where you make regular deposits, minimize withdrawals, and receive a return on your investment.

Deposits into the *relationship bank* start with doing the LITTLE THINGS to demonstrate interest and concern for others. Here are a few suggestions:

- Send an email just to say hello.
- Call to see how someone's son or daughter performed in an activity.
- Send a card or email on a holiday or birthday to say you are thinking about them.
- Encourage them when they start a new project.
- Express appreciation through a thank-you note or phone call.
- Compliment them for a job well done.
- Be supportive during times of struggle and grief.

LTM Challenge

Take a quick self-assessment. Do you currently give more than you expect to get? Or, are you preoccupied with waiting for people to do things to meet your needs or expectations?

Think about a significant relationship you have with someone, such as your spouse, close friend, parent, or child. Do you spend more time thinking about what they should be doing for you rather than what you could be doing for them?

Think about your job or whatever it is you do each day. What influences your decisions in this role? Which has priority—how the outcome will benefit you, or how it will benefit your employer, family, community group, or team?

> **Be intentional about investing more
> into your relationships than you withdraw.**

54. Break the Ice by Building Rapport

Have you ever talked to a person on the phone or met with someone for the first time and sensed that they felt uneasy? Were they reserved? Did they fidget and seem nervous or just a little awkward? If so, what did you do to break the ice?

In the course of our everyday lives, we will encounter people who may feel a bit uncomfortable the first time they meet us. Perhaps they don't know what to expect. They may be ill at ease in social situations, or nervous about making a good impression. Whatever the reason, your goal in all of these situations should be to make the person feel more relaxed and at ease.

If you sense that someone is uncomfortable during a phone conversation, try being casual and friendly. Engage in small talk before diving into the purpose of the call. Begin by asking a couple of ice-breaking questions that the other person will be comfortable answering. Throughout the conversation, smile and speak in an upbeat tone. By the end of the call, the person on the other end of the line will be appreciative of your efforts to make them feel more comfortable.

Meeting with someone for the first time in person presents a similar opportunity. Offer a warm and friendly greeting, a comfortably firm handshake, and make good eye contact. After you introduce yourself, proactively engage in small talk and ask some conversation-starting questions that demonstrate a sincere interest. Not only will this put the other person at ease, it will make them respect you as a person who genuinely cares and who desires to develop a sincere friendship.

LTM Challenge

Start to focus on what you can do to make people you've never met feel valued, appreciated, and comfortable. Go out of your way to show your interest in them.

If you are saying to yourself, *"I already do this,"* look for the refinements you can make to improve the rapport-building process. If you are striving for excellence to achieve your personal best, you can always get better.

Lastly, actively look for situations where people are uncomfortable such as the new employee, a first-time visitor to your club or organization, or someone standing off to the side at your next social event. Push yourself outside your comfort zone and make a new friend.

> **Building friendly relationships takes awareness,**
> **a strong desire to connect, and a concerted effort.**

55. Encourage Others With Your Words

One of my favorite quotes comes from the extraordinary public speaker and author, Cavett Robert. *"Three billion people on the face of the earth go to bed hungry every night, but four billion people go to bed every night hungry for a simple word of encouragement and recognition."*

Everyone needs to hear words of encouragement. When you encourage others, you lift their spirits, enhance their self-confidence, and add fuel to their motivational fire. Perhaps, more than anything, you give them hope and inspiration. If simple words of encouragement can do so much to enhance someone's life, why don't we do more of it? How long could it take? Ten seconds?

I went fishing a few weeks ago with an acquaintance. Kevin greeted me with a huge smile and said, *"The last time I went fishing with you, you said one of the nicest things anyone has ever said to me."* A little surprised, I asked him what he meant. He explained that I had paid him a great compliment by telling him how well he fought and eventually caught his 55-pound Amberjack.

Wow! I didn't remember giving him this accolade, but he sure did! Not only did he remember, he remembered it ten months later. Who would have thought a little compliment would make such a lasting impression?

Yesterday I was speaking with a young lady who has struggled with weight her entire life. She shared what she has been doing and the results she has had thus far. I told her how proud I was of her and encouraged her to continue despite her slow progress. She looked up with tears swelling in her eyes and told me how much she appreciated my words of encouragement. It was just one more reminder how our words of encouragement impact the lives of others.

In today's world, where people are so self-consumed with their own interests and desires, hearing words of encouragement are rare. While there are a lot of things you can do to strengthen your relationships with others, there are few things you can do or say that mean more to people than words of encouragement.

In the words of Zig Ziglar, *"You never know when a moment and a few sincere words can have an impact on a life."*

How about taking the time to offer some positive reinforcement or pay a compliment? Be intentional about looking for the good in others and telling them what you see. You may think someone doesn't need to hear an encouraging word, but they may be the ones who need it the most.

Do you have a parent, spouse, or significant other who needs a few words of encouragement? Do you have a child who aspires to win a race or a teenager who is hoping to be accepted to a certain college? Is an employee struggling to complete an assignment or monthly report? Perhaps your friend is down in the dumps and a word of encouragement from you is all he needs to change his mood.

Here are a few key points to remember when offering encouragement. Make it sincere, make it memorable, and speak from your heart. Why not surprise them with unexpected words that make them feel appreciated for what they do or who they are?

LTM Challenge

When you see people working hard to reach a goal, take ten seconds to encourage them. If you have seen progress in their pursuit, tell them what you have observed. Your words of encouragement may be just what they need to keep their dreams alive.

Comments like *"You're doing a great job," "Keep up the good work,"* or *"You rock!"* go a long way in making a difference in someone's outlook.

Make sure your words communicate your genuine feelings. While the words themselves are powerful, the feelings behind the words are what will be remembered. Before going to bed tonight, think of three people to encourage, recognize, or compliment. Just three. Will you do it?

> **When you look for the good in others**
> **and tell them what you see, you enhance**
> **their self-image and stand out in their minds**
> **as someone who noticed their efforts.**

56. The Word *Please* Gets Results

Most of us rely on help and assistance from others throughout our day—at work, home, and out in the community. In fact, we probably don't realize the extent to which we do. Every renowned leader will confirm that it's impossible to rise to the top without the efforts of others, and the way you ask for that help makes all the difference in the world. If you have children, you know how many times a day you have said: *"How do you ask?"* or *"What's the magic word?"*

At the most basic level, when we use the word *please*, it shows respect and consideration for the effort another person puts forth to help us. Including *please* with your request is not only a social norm but, if communicated with a smile and genuine sense of appreciation, it's a powerful way to establish rapport, build relationships, and develop your own character.

When we say *please*, people are more willing to fulfill our request or provide the help we need. As the adage goes, *"You have to give respect to get respect."* When you are polite and say *please*, people are more likely to respect you in return. And, without a doubt, your consistent use of *please* (with everyone, all the time) is a little thing that will most definitely make you noticeable in a crowd of busy people who are mindful only of their own selfish desires and personal To-Do lists.

Even for those of us who pride ourselves on good manners and almost always say *please*, it bears noting that how we say it really does matter. We should sound like we mean it and that we really do appreciate the assistance that someone else is providing.

LTM Challenge

This is a simple one. Use the magic word. Say *please* in all situations. Be conscious of how you say it. Smile and say it like you mean it!

> **The key to every successful relationship
> is putting the other person's needs ahead of your own.
> You can take a step toward stronger relationships
> every day with one simple,
> yet powerful word: *please*.**

57. Give the Gift of Appreciation

William James, well-known psychologist and philosopher, said, *"The deepest principle of human nature is a craving to be appreciated."*

We all want and need to feel valued for who we are and recognized for our contributions and accomplishments. We want to know that we have made a difference in someone's life. When we receive appreciation or recognition, it boosts our spirit, intensifies our passion, and reinforces our purpose. It builds our self-confidence and self-esteem. It gives us energy and motivates us to work harder and do more.

Benefits of Showing Appreciation

- When you give people a sincere compliment, words of encouragement, or just a warm smile, you are making their world a better place—in the home, at work, or in the community.

- When you express your approval or gratitude for something they have done, you not only enhance their lives, but you enrich yours as well. You feel more fulfilled because you have done something to make someone else's life better.

- It costs little or nothing to show our gratitude for things people do, and it almost always follows suit that they will demonstrate their appreciation for what you do.

- When you show an interest by noticing the good things others have done, they are instinctively drawn to you. It accelerates the relationship-building process and it also enhances their overall impression of you.

- Your value to the market escalates. When you show your appreciation to others, their respect for you grows and so does your influence as a leader. In today's world, people have choices. They absolutely prefer to work with people they like and trust and who show an interest in them.

- If you are in a leadership position, remember that people work harder and do more if they believe they will be recognized for their accomplishments. Show them you care and they will be loyal to you even if better opportunities come their way.

Six Ways to Demonstrate Appreciation

1. Be genuine about your praise and don't expect anything in return for being gracious.

2. Be very specific with your words and use the person's name whenever possible. This makes it more meaningful. For example, *"Bill, thanks for making us feel so welcome when we arrived at the hotel. It was the perfect start to our vacation."*

3. Establish eye contact and demonstrate positive body language. They go hand-in-hand with the words you choose.

4. Think of special ways to show your gratitude. For example, buy flowers or do something special for your spouse. You don't have to spend a lot of money for the thank-you to have value.

5. Send a handwritten thank-you card or note of appreciation. Because most people don't take the time to extend this simple gesture, those who do stand out.

If the praise or appreciation relates to a specific circumstance or a performance event, give it as soon after the event as possible to have the most impact. This is a LITTLE THING that makes a big difference.

LTM Challenge

I want to challenge you to make your expression of appreciation special so that you stand out as someone who genuinely cares. This includes the people whose job it is to serve you. It requires conscious effort on your part, but it's worth it.

And don't forget the simple LITTLE THINGS to let people know they are appreciated. For every handwritten thank-you note I write, I probably send 30 brief emails thanking people for the things they've done for me. For every gift I buy for my wife, I probably tell her 50 times how much I appreciate all she does for me.

Make a list of those people who regularly do things for you—your co-workers, friends, family members, team members, or employees—and determine how you can express your appreciation for the things they do for you. Be intentional about making everyone feel noticed and valued.

> **Showing your appreciation is a free form of currency.**
> **People will do more for recognition**
> **than they will for money.**

58. Make People Feel Good

One of life's simple but powerful truths is this: If you'll focus on others rather than on yourself, you'll make a positive difference in two lives—yours and the person with whom you interact. When you do things that make others feel good, it draws them closer to you and you to them.

It seems that in today's world most people are preoccupied with their own lives and problems. For this reason, when people go out of their way to do or say something that makes another person feel good, they stand out as people who value relationships.

Our lives offer endless opportunities to show people we truly care about them:

- In the workplace, making your co-workers feel good enhances the work environment, making it more enjoyable; it also increases your influence with them.

- In your business, making clients and customers feel appreciated draws them closer to you; it also increases your sales.

- In the home, it binds your family members closer together.

You've got the power to make someone else feel good. Need inspiration?

20 Ways to Show Someone You Care

1. Do your children's chores for the day.

2. Give your spouse or significant other a gift on your next date night or after they do something special for you.

3. Shovel snow for an older couple down the street, or cut the grass for a neighbor who is overwhelmed at work.

4. Call a friend going through a difficult period to show your support.

5. Send a client something special that made you think of him or her.

6. Send a gift basket or bouquet of flowers to the hotel room of a friend on a long road trip.

7. Invite a friend to dinner and plan an evening with his or her interest in mind.

8. Plan a special day with your kids, but don't tell them.

9. Offer to take a co-worker (who is not close to you) to lunch and buy it.

10. Plan a company or department meeting, surprising everyone with a party to show your appreciation for their hard work.

11. Pay the toll for a friend following you and tell the gate attendant to communicate your brief message.

12. Stop by the hospital to visit a friend.

13. Take dinner to a family suffering from financial hardship.

14. Stay late and help a co-worker finish an important project.

15. Call and invite an old friend to meet for coffee or tea.

16. Buy your friend sitting at another table in the restaurant a drink or dessert.

17. Go to the funeral of the loved one of a friend or co-worker.

18. Look someone in the eye and say how proud you are of him or her.

19. Say an encouraging word to your boss, teacher, coach, pastor, or priest. Leaders are lonely.

20. Offer to run an errand for an overworked friend.

LTM Challenge

Who do you love that you haven't communicated with lately? Which friend could use your support? Which co-worker needs a pat on the back? Take a moment and make someone's day special. It won't cost you anything, but the rewards are satisfying.

> **What sunshine and rain do for flowers,**
> **encouragement and kindness do for the human soul.**

59. Master the Art of Apology

Apologizing is not as simple as saying, "I'm sorry." Thoughtful and genuine apologies repair and rebuild relationships, but thoughtless or insincere apologies may do more harm than good.

Think of the last time you apologized for something you said or did. What words did you speak? Were they heartfelt and honest? Did your voice tone and body language send the same message as your words? Were excuses and justifications mixed in with your apology?

The way in which we apologize says a lot about our character. Do we accept full responsibility for the things we say and do, or do we feel the need to explain the reason for our actions by pointing fingers? Do the words coming out of our mouths have real meaning, or are we just apologizing because it's expected?

We all make mistakes. No one's perfect. But how we rebound from those mistakes and apologize for our behavior will play a critical role in the impressions we make and the respect we receive from our friends, family, and co-workers.

Someone wisely said that *a bend in the road is not the end of the road...unless you fail to make the turn.* If done correctly, your apology will restore a relationship and make a positive impression; distinguishing you as someone who accepts responsibility for your actions.

My wife and I have four children. So you can imagine there have been numerous times when we've had to remind them about how to give a proper apology. The tips below are based upon the lessons we have taught our children over the years, and I give my wife full credit for helping all of us learn how to make things right.

Three things to remember when you apologize:

- **Don't justify your actions or make excuses.** Giving an explanation or justification when you apologize cheapens your apology.

  The best way to apologize is to accept responsibility for your actions and start with the obvious words, *"I'm sorry."* You may want to take it one step further and add, *"I was wrong."* This won't be easy. It takes a strong person to accept responsibility for his or her actions and not try to justify them. Blaming others undermines your apology.

- **Mean what you say.** Be genuine and honest, making sure your tone and body language are consistent with the words you speak. If you try to fake an apology, people will see right through it, and it will only make the situation worse.

  If you have done something you shouldn't have done or said something you shouldn't have said, you have made a negative impression. An insincere apology is like pounding that negative impression into their head with a hammer. It's a sure way to lose respect.

  You may need a little time to pass in order to collect your thoughts before delivering a genuine apology, but don't let the clock run out. When you know you need to apologize, the sooner you can do it effectively, the better.

- **Ask for forgiveness.** After you have apologized, then seek forgiveness. Offer to make amends if appropriate. Hopefully the other person will forgive you, and you both can move on.

LTM Challenge

Who needs an apology from you? Do you have any damaged relationships? Make the call today to set up an appointment with someone whom you have wronged, offended, or misguided. Think about the words you will use and the way you will deliver those words. Will you accept the challenge?

When you have done or said something to hurt another person, you have a choice to make.
You can ignore it and let your relationship suffer the consequences, or you can make things right by offering a heartfelt apology.

---

60. Give Feedback the Right Way

When a toddler takes his first steps, Mom or Dad is most likely standing right there. If the little guy leans too heavily to one side, he is gently steadied. If he falls he is lifted up, praised, and encouraged to try again.

Providing constructive feedback to a friend, family member, or colleague is no different. Careful, consistent course correction is needed. Giving constructive feedback the RIGHT way is beneficial to both the receiver (improved performance, a shorter learning curve, and personal growth) and the giver (more respect, happier relationship, and better production).

The R.I.G.H.T. Way to Give Feedback

Give feedback and give it the right way. The acronym for the word RIGHT is an effective way to remember the essentials.

R. Respectful.   Showing respect for the other person is a fundamental principle for delivering any type of message, but it's especially important when it comes to giving feedback. People won't listen to feedback that is delivered aggressively, sarcastically or disrespectfully.

Ask permission to provide feedback. I like to ask those I coach or employ, *"If I see ways in which you can improve your performance, what would you like me to do?"* In most cases, they've said, *"By all means, tell me."* When I see things important enough that need correction, I begin by saying, *"Maria, you told me you wanted me to tell you when I noticed things that you could do to improve your performance."* In a respectful way, I explain how she can improve her results. As the relationships deepen and people begin to value my feedback, I don't need to tiptoe. They know I want the best for them and are almost always open to hearing the LITTLE THINGS they can do to improve.

If you have not asked for permission in advance, you could say, *"Would you be open to hearing some feedback on your report?"* Asking permission won't take much time and goes a long way to communicate your respect for the other person's time and efforts.

If what you have to say could be perceived by anyone listening as reflecting negatively on the other person, his or her work, or reputation, your conversation should be held in private.

I. **Issue Specific.** Keep your feedback message centered on the performance or issue that needs to be corrected—not the person or personality. It's very easy for an individual who is receiving feedback to become defensive, so do your best to stay focused on the specific issue that needs to be improved.

G. **Goal Oriented.** One of the objectives of constructive feedback is to improve performance. By including a discussion of goals in your feedback, you provide something practical and constructive on which to focus. In working with entrepreneurs, I remind them of their goals and help them see how they will be more likely to achieve them if they make the refinements I am suggesting.

If you are in management, the goals could include those of the company, department, team, or project. You could also remind your people that when they do the little things to get better, they are increasing their value to the company and to the marketplace.

H. Helpful. By giving constructive feedback, you can help someone become a better performer or a better person. As much as possible, use a helpful tone and show your support by recognizing the person's efforts. Offering praise and giving credit where credit is due will ensure that an individual will be more receptive to hear your feedback. Oftentimes I sandwich my constructive criticism between two positive or encouraging statements.

Another approach is to ask questions that will elicit self-discovery such as, *"How do you feel you did on this project?"* or *"How do you think you could have performed at a higher level?"* This generally leads to a less defensive and more productive conversation.

After you have expressed your sentiments and provided constructive feedback, make it a point to check back with the person within a few days to ensure that the relationship is intact. Find out if they have been hurt by your conversation, are harboring ill feelings, or are avoiding you.

T. Timely. Feedback is most valuable when it is delivered as soon as possible—while the event or performance issue is fresh in everyone's mind. Business and life move at a pace that seems to always be increasing. In order for your feedback to have a real impact, it needs to be fresh and relevant.

If people sense that you care and want them to succeed, it's much more likely that they will be appreciative of your comments and take them to heart.

LTM Challenge

Giving constructive feedback is a skill that managers and leaders work hard to perfect. The next time you are presented with the privilege to do so, I hope you'll use these key principles and feel confident that you can deliver better feedback.

> **When people can tell that you genuinely care**
> **about their best interests,**
> **they will be more receptive to what you have to say.**

61. What Bugs You?

Recently, I posed a straightforward question on the *Little Things Matter* Facebook page: What are the things people do that bug you? More people responded to this post than any other since launching this page. I had hit a nerve. Not surprisingly, the hot buttons were people who lie, are intentionally deceitful, or flaunt arrogance. The most common theme by far was lack of consideration for others.

Do you ever roll your eyes, bite your tongue, or blow your horn when people do any of these things?

- Drive 10 MPH below the posted speed limit
- Drive too close to you

- Flick their cigarette butts out the window
- Talk loudly in restaurants
- Call only when they want something
- Get drunk and become obnoxious
- Don't respond to emails, texts, and calls
- Interrupt while you're talking
- Scan their phone or computer for messages during a conversation
- Are late for calls and appointments
- Eat or chew gum with their mouth open

The number and nature of these responses prompted me to think about the ramifications of doing things that annoy people.

When you have a habit that bothers other people and do nothing about it, you brand yourself as someone who is inconsiderate. Being identified as a thoughtless and insensitive person is an undesirable characteristic; one that you would not want associated with your personal brand. Think about it. Do inconsiderate people attract or repel others?

I recognize that there is a group of people who have the attitude, *"This is a free country, so what if you don't like what I'm doing."* My life experiences have taught me that this type of thinking will cause you to end up unloved, unappreciated, unpopular, and unhappy.

The first step toward ridding yourself of distasteful or offensive habits is to identify them. Many of the things that people view as offensive are things we don't even consciously consider. As an example, your constant humming in the office could be annoying to everyone within earshot of you.

The easiest way to learn about what bugs people is simply to ask them. It may be awkward, but I guarantee you'll be held in high regard as someone who wants to improve. And believe me, most people will be only too happy to tell you what bugs them.

LTM Challenge

Start with your spouse, or another family member. Ask them to honestly tell you what bugs them. Use self-control to remain calm. Don't get defensive—that's a sure way to end the conversation.

When you're ready and feel secure enough, ask a trusted colleague, supervisor, or co-worker to tell you about your little habits that annoy them. If you just can't bring yourself to ask anyone directly, try this. Fill in the blanks: If I asked _____ to identify the one thing I do that really bugs them, they would say _____.

Make a conscious effort to watch how others are viewing your actions and reactions. Notice when others seem to be turned off by something you say or do. Start thinking about how you can be more considerate of others.

> **There are very few things more damaging to your personal brand than doing things that irritate people.**

62. The Dark Side of Sarcasm

Your day at work starts with a co-worker talking loudly on his phone to his girlfriend. When he hangs up, someone says, "*I think you should talk a little louder next time—the entire office didn't hear the details about last night's date.*"

Though it's often camouflaged as humor, sarcasm is really a convenient way to express criticism, disapproval, or hurt feelings without saying what's actually on your mind. An occasional off-the-cuff remark can easily escalate to an inappropriate and offensive conversational style.

The word *sarcasm* comes from an ancient Greek word meaning "to tear flesh." A few decades ago, sarcastic remarks were called cut-lows. Both the origin of the word and the slang expression illustrate the potentially damaging effects of sarcasm and reinforce my belief that sarcasm does not belong in our social and business interactions.

Unfortunately, sarcasm is all around us. Television sitcoms—often loaded with sarcastic remarks—are intentionally written for you, the viewer, to laugh at the character's embarrassment. Don't be fooled into thinking that these are merely clever sayings mouthed by quick-witted individuals. Television writers think they are entertaining the audience, but they are really setting an example for viewers to follow. Sadly, our children grow up believing that the risk of alienating another person in the interest of getting a laugh is socially acceptable.

One might argue, "*Sarcasm is okay with good friends. Life doesn't have to be so serious. Anyway they know we are just joking.*" I say, why take the chance? You never know the impact your words might have. What you think is an innocent poke may hit them at the wrong time and have a negative effect. It's a risk that I'm unwilling to take.

Although an occasional sarcastic remark may seem harmless, remember that people judge your character every day by what you say and how you act. The collective result of those judgments is your reputation.

Let me urge you to have courage to say what you really mean. In the earlier example, a person who values relationships would privately say in a caring way, *"Hey, I just want you to know that everyone could hear your conversation."* If you were the one who spoke so loudly, who would you respect more?

I won't sugarcoat it; sarcastic speech is a very difficult habit to break once you've allowed it to be part of your communication style and personal brand. And it's especially tough if the people around you thrive on the temptation of "one-upping" each other when it comes to sarcastic comments. The truth is sarcasm breeds sarcasm.

LTM Challenge

Here are a few tips to help you break free from the destructive habit of sarcasm:

- Start noticing the reactions of the victims of sarcasm. What are the immediate consequences? The victims may act like it was okay, but watch to see if they get quiet when someone changes the subject. This awareness alone will be a powerful motivator to change your own behavior.

- Think before you speak. Use a filter and consider how your words will be received.

- Apologize to people you may have offended with sarcastic or cutting remarks. Tell them you are working to eliminate sarcasm from your speech.

- Enlist a trusted friend or family member who is willing to enter a sarcasm-free zone with you. Agree that you will hold each other accountable by letting the other person know when they have been sarcastic.

> **Sarcasm is often hurtful and offensive**
> **to both the victim and the listeners.**
> **Though sarcasm may seem funny at the moment,**
> **the results are neither comical nor temporary.**

63. Defuse the Ticking Time Bomb

Have you ever thought or said something like this? *"If he does that one more time, I am going to lose it!"* Or, *"If she keeps treating me that way, I am going to give her a piece of my mind!"* Or, *"If this happens again, I won't be able to restrain myself!"*

These are examples of what I call the *ticking time bomb*. When people say these types of things, I cringe and want to say, "WARNING!" When you know in advance that you are going to retaliate if someone does or says something again, you are in danger of exploding, hurting other people, and damaging your reputation.

Losing control of your emotions is something that can happen anywhere—at home, in the workplace, or even on the volleyball court. My guess is we've all been there at one time or another. Whether it's a rare occurrence for you or something you struggle with regularly, it is critical that you never allow yourself to *lose it*.

When you lose control of your emotions and explode at someone, you damage your reputation in the eyes of the person who received the brunt of your anger and also in the eyes of witnesses as well. You can spend years building your reputation and ruin it in five seconds if you don't learn how to control your negative emotions.

Consider this true story as another type of a ticking time bomb.

A loyal reader of the *Little Things Matter* blog sent me an unusually curt and caustic email criticizing a recent post. I was a bit stunned when I read it, as I generally think of him as even-tempered, discerning, and complimentary. I thought to myself, *"What the heck is going on here?"* I sent him a short email to ask what he didn't like about the lesson. His response was enlightening and is worthy of a direct quote.

"I was sitting on another cross-country flight, not in a very good mood, and did not like the long description in the example you provided, nor did I think it proved your point. Todd, I know and respect you very much. We are friends. However my language should not have been as glib and unkind as it was. We all know the Reply button can be a time bomb and I hit it! I apologize. I learned a great lesson about keeping my mouth shut when I am tired and ornery."

I am sure you have found yourself in this type of situation as well. You're tired, frustrated, overwhelmed, or feeling resentful, and someone's behavior makes you want to scream. You feel the pressure building and unless you take precautionary measures, the ticking time bomb will get the best of you.

LTM Challenge

The next time you feel the tension rising and you start to think you can't handle any more of someone or something, take a deep breath and exhale slowly. Pause to consider the damage you might cause to your job, reputation, or relationship if you don't keep your emotions in check. Use this awareness to make sure you don't say or do anything you will later regret.

> **When you choose to respond
> rather than react to a difficult situation,
> you demonstrate to others and yourself
> that you are in control of your emotions.**

64. Don't Steal the Show

Are you annoyed when someone thoughtlessly cuts you off in traffic? How about when you've been waiting patiently in a long line at a ticket counter and someone waltzes right in and slips ahead of you to go to the front of the line? Doesn't it make you just want to say *"Hello!"* with a sarcastic tone or ask, *"What makes you think you're more important than I am?"*

It's no different when it comes to communication. There's nothing more frustrating than when someone barges in and imposes their agenda on us by offering a similar experience to the one we are sharing. For example, if a friend is excited to tell you about his deep-sea-fishing adventure where he caught an 80-pound yellowfin tuna, resist the temptation to tell him about the 90-pound tarpon you landed in the local fishing tournament. Let him enjoy the moment and fully share his experience. Don't take over the conversation by drawing the attention away from him and his story. In other words, don't steal the show.

Likewise, if someone you know is going through a difficult time and they share their grief with you, there's no need to interject how you felt when you experienced something similar. Simply allow the person to communicate their feelings. Listening quietly is actually the best way to show you care about the person.

No one intends to be a show stealer. On the contrary, people actually believe that it helps build rapport to relate in this manner. The following distinction keeps you from stealing the show: *relate to the person, not the moment.* To accomplish this, give the gift of listening—listening with genuine interest and without barging in, cutting them off, or stealing the show.

LTM Challenge

Consider these suggestions to avoid stealing the show:

- Listen to the conversations going on around you to hear what show stealing sounds like. You will be amazed at how common it really is! Pay specific attention to the person whose joy or experience is being robbed. Notice the facial expression, the body language, and the overall demeanor.

- Focus on listening more and talking less. Most successful people are able to control their tongues. An occasional, sincere response along the lines of *"Wow, that is amazing,"* or *"I'm proud of you,"* or *"I'm so sorry you're going through this"* will be welcomed.

- The next time someone shares an experience with you and you feel the need to comment, ask yourself, *"Am I about to steal the show?"* If you are, use self-control and resist the temptation. When the conversation has concluded and you have successfully withheld your comment or story, take a moment to recognize that you have done the right thing. Doing so is a great way to reinforce this LITTLE THING that matters.

> **One of the most effective ways to connect with people is to listen intently and avoid interrupting as they tell their experiences.**

65. Show an Interest in People's Things

Recently at a public speaking engagement, I exchanged business cards with numerous people. Because I had put a great deal of time and energy into creating my *Little Things Matter* business card, I noticed people's reactions when I gave them one. Some folks immediately put it into their pocket or wallet without even looking at it; others studied it momentarily. In some cases, they asked a question or said something complimentary about my card.

The way I responded to these people is most interesting. I found myself attracted to the people who took an extra five seconds to look at my business card, and I was feeling slightly offended by those who had no interest in looking at it.

Here's the really intriguing part. My reactions were instinctive. I didn't realize that my impressions were being formed so quickly and that I was looking for a certain reaction when I handed someone my card.

In fact, it wasn't until I read a *Success Magazine* article on the airplane trip home that I realized what had happened. The March 2010 issue featured an interview with Mark Jeffries, author of *What's up with your handshake?*

Discussing how to build rapport, Mark said,

> *You have to make the other person feel great about their communication with you. Don't put some-one's business card in your pocket. They are handing you a little life story. If you don't take a moment to look at the card, acknowledge it and say something about it, you are*

missing a huge opportunity to tilt the scales in your favor. This is one differentiator point, but it could be all you need to get into positive territory.

WOW!

Thinking this through, I began to analyze my business card exchanges over the weekend. He described exactly how I felt. Without realizing it, I was attracted to the people who showed an interest in my card and turned off by those who did not.

There were two big take-aways from this experience.

First, our opinions and thoughts are often formed at the subconscious level and our reactions become instinctive. As an example, generally if you greet people with a smile and a firm handshake, they will instinctively be drawn to you. But I doubt they consciously think: I like your smile and handshake.

This is perfect example of why LITTLE THINGS matter. Everything we do or don't do makes an impression. The more positive impressions we make, the more likable and respected we become.

Second, there is value to showing an interest in the things that are important to other people, even something as simple as their business cards. I must admit that even though I have focused on the LITTLE THINGS for more than two decades, I had never thought about taking the time to show an interest in someone's business card. At times, I've been the guy who barely looked at someone's card and just put it in my pocket.

LTM Challenge

Start noticing the things that are important to others and show your interest in them by saying something nice. It could be their new car, outfit or haircut; the paintings or photographs in their home or office; their pets and children; their neatly manicured lawn or newly planted flowers.

The next time you receive someone's business card, take the time to really look at it. Perhaps you can compliment them on the logo or ask a question about their company. Demonstrate your interest and remember that five seconds is all it takes to make a positive impression.

> **When you show an interest in
> the things that are important to people,
> they will instinctively be drawn to you.**

66. Handling Difficult Conversations

Delivering unpleasant news, correcting misunderstandings, confronting a friend or family member, and dealing with hard-to-talk-about issues are the kinds of conversations most of us dread. They're a part of life, however, and we can't avoid them. Although you may never be totally comfortable in these situations, there are a number of things you can do to make these necessary talks as productive and painless as possible.

Even the most challenging conversations can lead to an improved state of affairs for all involved if handled calmly and with respect. When you practice the art of handling difficult conversations, your interpersonal communication skills improve, your ability to influence others grows, and so does their respect for you.

Here are ten guidelines to help you confront challenging situations:

1. **Choose the right time and place.** If you are initiating the conversation, consider the "emotional climate." Don't hold the conversation when the other party is upset or angry. Respect his or her privacy by minimizing the chance of being overheard. Whenever possible, have these conversations face-to-face.

2. **Anticipate that you may not be on the same page.** Different perceptions of intent, interpretations of the facts, and judgment about what is right or best are usually at the root of all sensitive conversations. Keeping this in mind limits surprises. Remember, what may be logical to you make not be logical to others.

3. **Use a respectful tone.** The tone in which you communicate is as important as what you say. Speak calmly with kindness and respect. Your tone should reflect your willingness for a good outcome, which increases the likelihood that your message will be received in the manner in which it is intended.

4. **Genuinely desire a win-win outcome.** If you begin the conversation with the intent to win the other party to your point of view, you'll often be disappointed. Instead, aim for a compromise or resolution that satisfies your goal and meets the needs of the other person.

5. **Be empathetic.** Try to understand the point of view as well the emotional state of the other person. Ask questions to learn their perspective. Understanding the other party's position helps you make better decisions regarding how to address the situation. I have found that, in most cases, the other person is aware of what happened and usually accepts responsibility to correct the situation. When you show genuine interest in understanding the other person's side of the story, you are more effective in resolving the matter.

6. **Maintain eye contact.** As in any constructive face-to-face communication, maintaining eye contact helps you gauge the receptivity of the other person throughout the conversation and demonstrates your interest in what is being said.

7. **Stay in control.** If you express anger, it is natural for the other person to respond accordingly to match your emotional state. If at all possible, don't begin the conversation until you are in control of your emotions and then do whatever it takes to remain calm.

8. **Write it out.** If time permits, it is helpful to put the details of the situation in writing. Include what you wish both parties to achieve. Doing so gives you an opportunity to consider all views and nuances of the situation. Taking the time to properly prepare for any important conversation yields better results.

9. **Don't interrupt.** When the other person is speaking, never interrupt. Show the other person the respect you want to be shown when you are talking. In addition, don't appear to be anxious to respond. People who can't wait to speak generally aren't listening because they are so focused on what they want to say.

10. **Don't team up.** Avoid saying things like, *"Everyone in the department feels the same way,"* or *"I have heard about this from countless people."* When I hear these kinds of statements, I immediately discount what is being said because in most cases they are exaggerations. If there is an issue that needs to be addressed, resist the temptation to strengthen your position by including others. If the issue is so serious that you need to bring others into the discussion, make sure they are present.

LTM Challenge

If you are a person who dislikes confrontation, difficult conversations of any nature can be stressful. You can, however, be proactive in reducing this stress when you accept that such conversations are inevitable from time to time and that you can improve your skills in dealing with them by putting some of the above recommendations into practice.

Finally, don't try to resolve your conflicts through email. This is a cowardly approach. Instead, push yourself out of your comfort zone, pick up the phone, and schedule an appointment to meet if at all possible. If scheduling an appointment to meet is not possible, then have the discussion over the phone.

While no one likes having difficult conversations, avoiding them is seldom the answer.

> **When you show respect for the other person and genuinely desire a positive outcome, difficult conversations won't be so painful.**

67. Living Beyond Ourselves

Never in my life have I seen more selfishness than I see today. I am witnessing a higher percentage of people who leave shopping carts in parking spaces next to their cars, who hardly acknowledge the store clerks serving them, who won't return a phone call or email, who don't R.S.V.P for a party, or who insist on being the center of attention. It's as though people are living in their own self-serving cocoons with little regard for what's going on around them.

The good news is that, for those of us who want to attract success into our life by achieving our personal best, we can stand out from the crowd by putting the interests of others before our own.

Zig Ziglar, arguably one of the best sales trainers of our day, said, *"You can have everything in life that you want if you will just help enough other people get what they want."*

When I think of people who are unselfish, here are the words that come to mind: generous, considerate, kind, likable, friendly, trusted, caring, thoughtful, fair, respected, honest, patient, authentic, and benevolent. It's interesting to see how many of the attributes required for success go hand-in-hand with selflessness. Take a few minutes to think of the unselfish people you know. Do they have those positive traits as well?

Assuming that our natural tendency is toward selfishness, we must be intentional about putting others first. Your daily routine literally presents hundreds of opportunities.

Here are some ideas to open your mind to the endless possibilities available to us:

- When you take out your gum or mints, offer one to those around you before helping yourself.

- As you walk through doorways, smile, hold the door open and say something nice to the people, even if you have to wait for them to pass through the doorway.

- When you are walking and someone is going to cross your path, stop, acknowledge the person, and let him or her go first.

- If you live in a home with other people, keep your belongings picked up so other family members don't have to see them or clean up on your behalf.

- If you work in an office, keep your personal work area clean and do your part to make sure the overall work environment is one that all of your co-workers can appreciate.

- When driving, show courtesy to the drivers around you.

- When sending emails, take an extra few seconds to show an interest in people.

- When having conversations with people, listen more and talk less. Wait patiently for the opportunity to speak.

- If you have friends or family members going through a difficult period, pick up the phone and tell them how much you appreciate them and offer a word of encouragement.

LTM Challenge

I encourage you to be aware throughout the day of opportunities to be unselfish and then to act on those opportunities.

Then there's the chance to take your selflessness to a higher level. Millions of people need food, shelter, healthcare, and protection from abuse. Count your blessings and give from your heart: time, money, or both.

> **When you put the needs, desires, and interests**
> **of others before your own,**
> **you will develop deeper friendships,**
> **people's respect for you will grow,**
> **and you will feel better about the person**
> **you are becoming in the process.**

68. People Are as Different as They Look

If you want to build relationships based on mutual respect, you must recognize and value the diversity in people. The fact is we all come from a variety of backgrounds, religions, and nationalities. We each have distinguishing features, life experiences, education, political leanings, personality type, and family upbringing. Because no two people are alike, these differences shape our perceptions and the way we view the world.

Far too often I have been part of group discussions and witnessed people who quickly dismissed the ideas of others. Whether their disagreement was communicated through the words they spoke or through their body language, it was clear that they disagreed.

Dismissing an idea just because it didn't originate from your thought process is a sign of arrogance. In reality the ability to think differently can spark creativity and innovation. Elbert Hubbard—an American philosopher, writer and publisher of the 19th century—reinforced why we should be receptive to the ideas of others. *"The recipe for perpetual ignorance is: be satisfied with your opinions and content with your knowledge."*

Valuing the differences in people also helps you become a more effective communicator. Tony Robbins described it this way:

> *To effectively communicate we must realize we are all different in the way we perceive the world and use this understanding as a guide to our communication with others.*

Being open to the perspectives of others enhances your listening skills, demonstrates your sincere interest in the other person, and helps you better connect with others. All of these skills are required to build long and meaningful relationships.

LTM Challenge

I hope that after reading this lesson you will not only intellectually accept the idea that we are all different, but you will also value the contributions from others. Here are my challenges for you.

- Be less critical of others. Instead, acknowledge and learn to appreciate people as unique individuals.

- Disagree without offending. When you find yourself disagreeing with another person, pause and recognize that they are sharing their views based on their life experiences, which are unlike yours. Respect their opinions even though you may disagree. If you can't reach an agreement, agree to respectfully disagree.

- Value the uniqueness of people when discussing ideas. Show respect by listening intently to what they have to say and learn as much as you can about their ideas or plans. Who knows? Their ideas may be better than yours.

> **Enrich your life by expanding your mind,**
> **valuing other people's opinions**
> **and learning new ideas.**
> **Above all, appreciate the beauty of our differences.**

69. Use Preferred Methods of Communication

The November 2009 issue of *Success Magazine* reported the results of a readership survey concerning communication.

The question was: *"What is your preferred method of communicating?"* Here are their answers:

- 3%Text Messaging
- 5% Social Media
- 13% Phone
- 39% Face-to-face
- 40% Email

Let's look at the demographics of the 950 people who responded. The mean household income was $126,300 compared to the national index of $73,600; over 50 percent were self-employed compared to the national index of 6.4 percent, and 89 percent have a college education compared to the national index of 60.7 percent.

What can we learn from this data?

- The respondents were above average in income, education, and initiative.

- The glaring statistic here is that only three percent of the respondents prefer communicating via text messaging. It's not surprising when you think about how texting works and the disruption it can produce in a workday. Every time a text message is sent, an interruption occurs—a thought process, a business meeting, or conversation—and every interruption stifles productivity.

- It's not surprising that email was chosen as the most popular method of communication. It certainly is the most time efficient because you can determine when to respond. You can return emails during scheduled blocks of time. Using email prevents interruptions from non-urgent calls and text messages. Most of us can type much faster on the computer keypad than on a cell phone keypad. It allows busy people the flexibility to communicate during non-business hours.

- Of course, face-to-face is the best when time and scheduling permit.

I have observed that most people initiate communication with their preferred method. It's wise then for us to do the same when communicating with them. If people prefer to talk on the phone, call them. If they would rather get together face-to-face, suggest a meeting. If they send an email, hit *Reply* instead of picking up the phone. Modeling someone's behavior is a good way to accelerate the rapport-building process.

Although email is the most convenient and productive way for me to communicate, I am cautious about using it exclusively. There are occasions when email just doesn't do the trick—either because the subject is too complex, or it's an emotionally charged issue, or I just want to hear the person's voice—so I pick up the phone or get together with them.

LTM Challenge

Determine your preferred method of communication and rationale for using it. Be intentional about communicating with people using their preferred method. Avoid sending text messages to people in a business environment unless you know they prefer texting.

> **Using someone's preferred method of communication is one of the LITTLE THINGS that matter in building relationships.**

70. Communicate Clearly and Concisely

Have you ever read a long email and said to yourself, *"When is this person ever going to get to the point?"* Or, just as painful, have you listened to someone talk for ten minutes and felt completely lost as to why the person called and where he or she was going with the conversation?

What these people don't realize is that rambling emails and incoherent conversations undermine their ability to reach their goals personally and professionally. The truth is that other people don't have time to ferret out a message nor do they want to play guessing games to figure out what it is you're trying to say. Either they press *Delete* or they tune you out before the conversation is over.

It's easy to see that we need to develop good communication skills if we want to build a successful career and maintain healthy relationships. Three things are necessary:

1. Be clear about your message: What do you want to get across? Is the information useful and accurate?

2. Understand who your audience is and how they will receive your message.

3. Deliver that message as concisely as you can without people viewing you as being abrupt or unfriendly.

Whether it's personal or business, be clear and concise in all your communication every day and everywhere. Be conscious of every email, letter, or report you write, or comments you make on social media sites. Be mindful of what you say in telephone conversations or at luncheon meetings.

Always be cognizant that your communication style plays an essential role in developing your brand, establishing market value, and contributing to your likability factor.

LTM Challenge

Become aware of all your communications and consider how you can most effectively convey your thoughts in a clear, direct, and friendly manner without being misunderstood.

In order to enjoy healthy relationships, it's critical that we improve our communications skills. Starting with the next email you type, ask yourself the following three questions:

- Is it friendly?
- Is it clear?
- Is it concise?

When you next engage in a conversation, ask yourself the same three questions:

- Am I friendly?
- Am I clear?
- Am I concise?

> **Learning to clearly communicate your points in a friendly manner using the fewest number of words possible is a skill worth mastering.**

71. How to Avoid Misunderstandings

Early in my career I found myself involved in countless situations that resulted in misunderstandings. My natural reaction was to blame others rather than accept responsibility. After years of misunderstandings (often resulting from wrong assumptions), I made the decision that I would accept 100 percent responsibility for all my communications with others.

The decision to accept this responsibility has forced me to become a more effective communicator and has improved my ability to identify warning signs where there may be a breakdown in communication.

I would like to share with you six lessons I've learned about how to avoid misunderstandings.

1. **Make sure written communication is clear.** Always read your written or typed messages and ask yourself, *"How could this message be misunderstood?"* This extra time is worth the investment in your brand. I review just about every email I send and in many cases I am able to refine and clarify my message. The more you focus on the clarity of your communication, the better communicator you become.

2. **Evaluate the clarity of your oral communications.** Whether you're having a casual conversation with a friend, giving someone directions, leaving a voicemail message, or providing instructions to a business colleague, focus on the clarity of your oral communications. Look for signs of confusion, such as a quizzical look, or the same question restated more than once.

3. **Write things down and repeat them.** Write down all instructions that are given to you. Whether you are going to the grocery store for your parents or spouse, ordering take-out food for the family, or working on an important project, always write everything down. Writing things down helps you remember and reduces stress in the process. Take one additional step: repeat the instructions to the person who gave them to you to ensure accuracy.

4. **Watch for potential misunderstandings.** When you choose to accept full responsibility for all misunderstandings, something interesting will happen. You begin to see warning signs that you have previously overlooked. It may be a facial expression, a comment made, or distractions in the background that alerts you to the possible miscommunication.

5. **Confirm all details and put them in writing.** When a task or event is my responsibility, I confirm all the details in writing. If I have a call scheduled, I confirm the date of the call, the time of the call, the time zone if appropriate, and who is responsible for initiating the call. Once it's confirmed, I put it in my calendar.

6. **Ask others to repeat what they have heard.** Ask people to repeat your instructions. You might say, *"Bob, before we wrap up this call, can you please confirm your responsibilities as part of this project?"* Repetition forces them to articulate your directives in their own words. It also clarifies whether or not you have been understood.

LTM Challenge

Starting today, accept full responsibility for all misunderstandings. Don't allow yourself to play the blame game. When you are involved in a misunderstanding, analyze what you could have done to avoid it and learn from the experience. Determine if you ran past any warning signs.

> **Avoiding misunderstands increases your value to the market, enhances the respect from others, and enables you to lead more effectively.**

72. Good Emails Support Your Brand

Email has become people's preferred method of communication, trumping face-to-face, phone communication, social sites, and texting. It's wise then to evaluate how you are branding yourself through your emails. The way you communicate through email with your boss, co-workers, clients, prospective employers, and even your friends will have a significant impact on how you are viewed.

What's your email brand? Have you given it any thought?

Take a few seconds to think of someone who is very friendly in their emails. What's your impression of this person? Now think of someone who sends one-line emails and doesn't take the time to offer a few friendly words either at the beginning or end of the email. What impression has this person made on you?

Writing Better Emails

Remember that, no matter how insignificant these tips may seem, everything matters when you want to achieve your personal and professional best.

1. **Take time and have pride.** Every email you send makes an impression and plays a role in defining your overall brand. Take a few extra minutes to make sure your emails are properly composed and reflect a sincere and friendly personality; it's time well spent.

2. **Return emails.** Failing to return emails or neglecting to return them in a timely manner will brand you as inconsiderate or irresponsible. Most people expect a response within 24 hours. If that's not possible, make those times the exception rather than the norm.

3. **Use proper names.** People love to hear and see their names. Take time to type a person's name, rather than just an initial, and include a greeting, like *"Hi,"* or *"Hey,"* or *"Good morning,"* or something appropriate for that person.

4. **Be friendly.** The demeanor you project in your online communication should reflect your personality. If you value your relationships, take an extra 15 seconds to type something friendly

at the beginning or end of the email. It can as be simple as *"I hope you had a relaxing weekend,"* or *"Thanks for all you do."*

5. **Be clear and concise.** Say what you need to say as clearly as you can, using the fewest number of words possible. No one likes or has time for long, rambling or confusing emails that they have to read more than once to understand.

6. **Proof your emails.** Never send an email without proofing it at least once. If it is important, read it two or three times to make sure you are pleased with the message. Look for missing words and misspellings that aren't picked up by the spell-check function such as "there" versus "their." Also consider how your message could be misunderstood.

7. **Acknowledge emails.** If you receive an email that you're not prepared to respond to for whatever reason, send a short message acknowledging the email and indicating when you will respond. Don't leave people wondering if you received their messages.

8. **Write short sentences.** Shorter sentences are easier to read and comprehend.

9. **Write short paragraphs.** Short paragraphs will be easier to read and will improve the likelihood of them being read. People often scan long paragraphs and miss important details of your message. Limit your paragraphs to two or three sentences and include a space between paragraphs.

10. **Cover multiple topics.** If your email covers more than one topic, separate the topics using numbers or bullets. This allows you to

logically convey your thoughts. It also makes it easier for the reader to follow your topics and respond separately to each point. Your other option is to send separate emails for each topic you want to cover.

11. **Be careful what you forward.** Everything you forward—jokes, inspirational quotes, or pictures—is a reflection of your personal brand.

12. **Be cautious.** If your emotions are flaring, allow a little time to let these emotions settle before pressing *Send.* Save the draft and hold it for a few hours or a day. You will be glad you did.

13. **Sign your email.** Take the extra two seconds to type your name at the end of your email.

14. **Use the recipient's time zone.** Avoid confusion when you are scheduling an appointment or a phone call. Use the time zone of your contact. This will keep them from trying to convert your time to their time zone, and it will reduce potential misunderstandings.

15. **Know when <u>not</u> to press *Reply All*—**If your response to an email is only directed to the person who sent the email, then don't press the *Reply All* button. Respect the time of the other parties and don't make them read and delete your email.

Email is a great way to efficiently communicate, but don't rely on it exclusively. Set a goal to talk to people at least once for every ten email exchanges. Relationships are best built in person, second by phone calls, and third by the written word. Take full advantage of the first two if you want the relationship to grow.

LTM Challenge

Scan the messages in your email *Sent* folder to evaluate if you have been portraying a positive email brand. Consider how you can make improvements to your email communication.

I invite you to download the free report for more email tips and strategies under the REPORTS tab at LittleThingsMatter.com.

> **Every email you send makes an impression and plays a role in defining your personal brand.**

73. Phone Greetings That Open Doors

We all make judgments about people the first time we see them, but this is also true the first time we hear them. One of the LITTLE THINGS we don't consciously think about is how to make a proper phone introduction. Your tone of voice and the words you speak create an impression. Make sure it's a positive one.

Because there is a difference in your greetings depending on the situation we will divide this discussion into two categories: business and social.

Calling a Place of Business

- When you call a business or organization and someone other than the person you are expecting answers the phone, introduce yourself in the following manner: *"Hi, my name is Tom White. May I please speak with Katy Williams?"*

- If you have a call previously scheduled with Katy, reference the appointment in your greeting by saying, *"Hi, my name is Tom White. I'm calling for Katy Williams. We have a two o'clock call scheduled."* By mentioning that you have a specific appointment, your call takes on a sense of appropriate urgency.

- If the person answering the phone uses his or her name in the greeting, you should take the time to repeat it. For example, the person answering the phone says, *"Thank you for calling ABC Widgets. This is Amber, how may I help you?"* Respond in a friendly tone, *"Hi Amber. My name is Tom White. How are you doing today?"* After exchanging pleasantries, ask, *"May I please speak with Katy Williams?"*

When you introduce yourself as described above, you stand out from all the other people who call. Being friendly and professional makes an impact. It's also important to recognize that the person answering the phone often has influence on the decisions made within a business or organization. Even if I call a utility company to report a problem, I've learned that being friendly and introducing myself properly often results in better service.

Introducing yourself is also a timesaver. Rather than having an exchange in which the person asks, *"May I tell her who's calling?"* and I have to respond with my name, I eliminate a step and save time for both of us. This may seem inconsequential, but I've learned that implementing hundreds of little time-management tips throughout your day compound for increased productivity.

Calling a Friend at Home

Here is what I recommend when calling someone's home.

- If the person you are calling answers the phone, begin by introducing yourself as part of a friendly greeting, such as *"Hi Mark. This is Tom White. How are you doing today?"* You never want someone to wonder who is calling.

- If the person you intend to speak with does not answer the phone, introduce yourself and engage in conversation before asking for the other person. As an example, if you are calling Mark Davy, but his wife Ann answers the phone, say in an upbeat and friendly manner, *"Hi Ann. This is Tom. How are you doing?"* After a short period of small talk, ask, *"Hey, is Mark around?"*

- If I make a call and I'm not sure that the person who answers is the one I want to speak to, I always introduce myself by saying, *"Hi, this is Todd Smith. Is Sherry available?"* Even if it turns out to be Sherry, I haven't offended her by asking. It's always better to play it safe.

Answering the Phone

- When you answer the phone, be proactive and introduce yourself as part of your greeting. Don't make people wonder who it is. I answer by simply saying, *"This is Todd."* Most of my successful friends answer their phones by using their first and last name. For example, Eddie's greeting is simply *"Eddie Stone,"* and Tina answers by saying, *"Hi, this is Tina Williams."*

- When I recognize the person's number or name on my phone, I answer, *"Hi, Beth. How are you doing today?"* If it's a close friend, I might use an informal greeting like, *"What's up, buddy?"*

- If you are a business owner, instruct all employees to answer the phone by introducing themselves within the first sentence and to speak in a professional and friendly manner. For example, *"Thank you for calling ABC widgets. This is Amber. How may I help you?"* This is a simple thing to teach your employees, and it will make a favorable impression on everyone who calls.

LTM Challenge

Over the next week, be mindful of your phone greetings. If you implement these tips you can be assured of making a positive impression on everyone you call and everyone who calls you. One more thing: remember to smile. ☺ People can hear your smile through your voice.

> **Your introduction and greetings on the phone**
> **can make a lasting impression and**
> **a positive contribution to your personal brand.**

74. Make Voicemail Work for You

Voicemail is a vital form of communication at home and at the office. The messages you leave play a small but important role in how you are viewed.

Consider these ten suggestions to make the most of your voicemail messages:

1. **Leave a message.** Current technology allows a person to see the details of a missed call. Accordingly, when you hear someone's voicemail, leave a message stating the purpose of your call. Why not? You had a reason for making the call in the first place. Leaving a brief message saves you time from having to call back later.

2. **Speak with energy in your voice.** How you sound on someone's voicemail makes a noticeable impression. Make that impression positive by sounding upbeat.

3. **Be prepared.** When you hear the phone ring four or five times, start thinking about the message you want to leave. Be clear and concise. You'll make a better impression and the return call will be more productive.

4. **Speak with a friendly voice.** You can smile and say something simple like, *"Hi Mike, this is Dan White calling. I hope you had a great weekend. The reason I am calling is_____."* After you finish your message, conclude your recording by saying something positive, such as *"I am looking forward to talking with you."*

5. **Let people know your availability.** Tell people when you can receive a return call. This will allow both of you to be more productive with your time.

6. **Leave a clear message.** There's nothing worse than a voicemail that only says, *"Call me."* If your message clearly states the purpose of the call, it gives the person time to think about it and helps them prioritize the timing of their return phone call. It also helps in the event you end up playing phone tag.

7. **Inform them if no return call is required.** If the subject of your call does not require a return call, give a detailed message and tell them it's not necessary to return your call. This is a time-saver for both parties.

8. **Repeat your phone number.** When leaving your phone number, always speak slowly, and give your phone number twice. Because most people aren't this thoughtful, this will certainly make a positive impression.

9. **Erase your mistake.** If you make a mistake in the recording of your message, finish your message as best you can. Then press either the star "✳" key or the pound "#" key. On most cell phone voicemail systems you hear a prompt that allows you to erase and re-record your message.

10. **Avoid leaving negative messages.** I believe it's best to discuss negative topics in person. When you need to talk about a negative subject, let people know the purpose of the call, but avoid leaving a message with the details of your feelings.

LTM Challenge

Start to be aware of the voicemail messages you leave. Consider your words and the tone of your voice. Remember that LITTLE THINGS matter, despite how trivial they may seem at the time.

> **Recording clear, efficient, and friendly**
> **voicemail messages identifies you**
> **as a thoughtful and considerate person.**

75. Project a Positive Image Over the Phone

If you stop to think about how much business is transacted over the phone in any given day, it's wise to be conscious of your telephone speaking voice, the words you use, and how you conduct yourself during a call.

Below are ten tips to help you make a positive impression.

1. **Prepare for the call.** Before making business calls, take the time to prepare. The more prepared you are for a call, the more confident you will sound. Jot down the topics you want to talk about or questions you need to ask.

2. **Begin by introducing yourself.** When you place a call, always start by introducing yourself to whoever answers the phone. Don't keep the person wondering who you are or why you are calling.

3. **Focus on your energy.** People who sound upbeat and positive make a better impression than those who don't. Be aware of your energy, voice tone, and speed. Sound like you are relaxed and unhurried, happy to be alive, and that you are genuinely pleased to be speaking to this person.

4. **Be friendly.** People are naturally drawn to considerate and likable people. Whether you are talking to a co-worker, friend, prospective client, or with the CEO of a company during an interview, sound friendly. When you speak with a smile on your face, an amiable tone, distinct pronunciation, and slow enough that the listener does not have to ask you to repeat something, people will be more likely to do business with you or your company.

5. **Make people feel comfortable.** When speaking with someone for the first time, you may sense that they are timid and apprehensive. Be sociable and pleasant to make them feel relaxed. This always results in a more productive conversation.

6. **Speak with a confident tone.** Whether you realize it or not, you are presenting your personal brand every time you have a conversation with someone. Before people will trust you, believe in you, or buy anything you have to offer, they must first buy you. However, they won't give credibility to what you are saying if you don't present yourself as a confident person.

7. **Follow the two-second rule.** Since you can't see the people speaking, it's hard to know if they are finished with their thought or just pausing to go on to the next sentence. So it's a good idea to wait two seconds to make sure they have finished. If you start to talk before they have finished, stop, and encourage them to finish before sharing what you have to say.

8. **Carry a notepad.** When I am conducting a business call, I often take notes. Sometimes these notes concern things that will be my responsibility after the call is finished. If I write them down I won't forget. On other occasions, I make notes of things I want to share or discuss when it is my turn to talk. Writing down my thoughts during the conversation enables me to focus on the subject rather than trying to remember what I want to convey when the other person stops talking. This also prevents me from jumping into the conversation prematurely.

9. **Avoid using a hands-free device.** If you are having an important conversation, speak directly into the phone rather than using a hands-free device. The problem with most hands-free devices is that it is harder for others to hear what you are saying. Background noise can be very distracting. If you don't want to hold the phone to your ear, purchase a high quality hands-free device.

10. **Avoid using a speakerphone.** Turning on your speakerphone can even be more annoying than using a hands-free device. Unless you are in a room with a group of people who are part of your conversation, don't use your speakerphone. Even if you are calling your best friend, show them the courtesy of talking directly into the phone.

LTM Challenge

Perform a self-evaluation when you are on the phone today. How would you rate your tone, speed, energy level, and etiquette?

Starting now, become intentional about how you present yourself in all your personal and business calls. Before long, most of the behaviors intended to help you project a powerful brand will become second nature to you.

> **How you present yourself over the phone**
> **is a reflection of your personal brand.**

76. Cell Phone Etiquette

Do you believe in cell phone etiquette? Or, more realistically, do you know the right thing to do but rationalize that it's okay *"just this once"* to talk on your cell phone while in line at the grocery store or to read a text message in the middle of a conversation with your friend? And before you know it, *"just this once"* becomes an irritating and disrespectful habit.

The gadget formerly known only for phone calls is now the "macdaddy" of technology. It allows a person to call, text, email, surf the web, and download music and videos, demanding an even greater need for rules of etiquette. If you don't show respect and common courtesy when using your cell phone, you run the risk of aggravating people and destroying your personal brand. On the other hand, if you use discretion and follow the simple recommendations outlined below, you will distinguish yourself from crowd by being thoughtful and considerate.

It's best to avoid using your cell phone when you are:

- **In public places.** When you are in public places where others can hear your conversation, avoid talking on your cell phone. If your phone rings, let it go into voicemail. If you determine it is absolutely critical to accept the call, be respectful of others. Walk outside or to a private area where others won't be annoyed or distracted by your conversation. If there is no escaping, keep your voice down and cover your mouth to keep your voice from traveling and wrap up the call as soon as possible.

- **Spending time with family.** Unless you have a job that requires you to be on call 24 hours a day, be respectful of your family by not talking, texting, surfing the web, or emailing when you are together. There will be occasions when an important call or message must be dealt with immediately, but try to keep those times to a minimum. When you do make an exception, apologize to your family members. The example we set for our children will pave their way to appropriate behavior.

- **Traveling with others in a car.** When you're spending time with people in a car, give them your full attention.

- **Driving.** For safety's sake, it's best to avoid talking on the phone while driving your car. And, of course, you should never email or text while driving.

- **At work.** If you use your cell phone for personal matters during the time you are paid to do your job, you are stealing from your employer. If there are personal calls, texts and emails that must be returned during your workday, do so during your break or lunch hour.

- **Attending presentations or religious services.** Nothing is quite as annoying to those sitting around you as hearing a long, musical tune playing out of your pocket or purse.

- **During meetings.** When you attend a meeting or share a meal with someone, put your phone on silent mode. Better yet, don't bring it into the meeting. Also, don't send a text or email or check your messages during the meeting. Even though your phone may not make sounds, your attention is diverted from people in attendance and is disrespectful. Besides, how can you concentrate on the discussion when you are typing or reading messages?

- **Spending time with friends.** Some of us don't have a lot of time to spend with friends. So when you are together, give them your undivided attention and enjoy the fellowship. You will very seldom see me with my phone when I am out socially. I want to thoroughly enjoy my experience and show respect for those who choose to spend time with me.

LTM Challenge

Don't let your cell phone become an addiction. Learn to control the times when it is used. Fifteen years ago, none of us had cell phones and we lived our lives just fine. Most things can wait until the time is appropriate to take the call or respond to the email or text. If you accept this challenge, your world becomes more enjoyable, your time management skills improve, you experience less stress, and the people around you feel more valued.

> **Show your respect by not sending texts,
> emails or talking on the phone
> when you are around other people.**

77. Record a Competent Voicemail Greeting

Over the years I've developed an aptitude to quickly and accurately read people. Selecting the right people with whom to do business has definitely played an important role in my professional success. There are many LITTLE THINGS I instinctively look for and notice; one that stands out is a person's voicemail greeting. A friendly greeting can make a positive impression; a goofy greeting can make a negative impression; an automated greeting is often viewed as impersonal and inconsiderate.

Here are five tips to record an impressive voicemail greeting:

1. **Identify yourself.** This enables your callers to confirm they have dialed the right number. When people use an automated greeting or when they don't include their name in their greeting, it leaves me wondering why. If you prefer to identify yourself with only your first name, that's acceptable on your personal cell phone or home voicemail. On a business line, however, I suggest including both your first and last name and your job title.

2. **Speak with energy.** When you record your voicemail greeting, speak as though you walk with a bounce in your step and are enjoying a successful life. People are instinctively drawn to people with positive attitudes. If you sound like you just woke up, it's more than likely you'll make a negative impression.

3. **Avoid overly creative greetings.** High-profile sales trainers often advise you to record unique or crazy greetings as a way to stand out. These creative greetings can sound corny or contrived and repeat callers quickly get tired of hearing this kind of message. If you want to be viewed as a professional, make sure your greeting presents you as one.

4. **Tell people what to do.** This is my personal greeting: *"Hi, you have reached the voicemail for Todd Smith. At the tone, please leave your name, phone number, the purpose of your call, and the best time to reach you. I will return your call as soon as possible. Thank you."*

   The voicemails I receive in response to this greeting allow me to use my time most productively, prepare for the return call or, if appropriate, send an email instead of returning the phone call. Knowing the purpose of the call also allows me to continue the communication through their voicemail if we end up playing phone tag.

5. **Refuse to use computer-generated greetings.** I think it is inconsiderate when people select a computer-generated message like, *"The person you are calling at 9-4-1-5-5-5-1-2-3-4 is not available to take your call, please leave a message at the tone."* When I hang up I am left wondering if I dialed the correct number. This requires me to take the time to verify that I've dialed the number correctly. Even then, I am sometimes left wondering if I wrote down the number correctly in the first place.

Bonus Tip: If you find that people get cut off before completing their message on your cell phone voicemail, call your carrier. For a small fee you can lengthen the time allotted for people to leave their messages.

LTM Challenge

Listen to your voicemail greeting on your home and business phones. What kind of impression are you making on your callers? Re-record if necessary, incorporating these simple tips.

> **Your voicemail greeting may be someone's first impression of you. Make sure it's a positive one.**

78. Discover Your Unique Gift

What do Wolfgang Amadeus Mozart, Michael Jordan, Warren Buffett, David Letterman, Roger Federer, Michael Jackson, Mary Kay Ash, Bill Gates, and Oprah Winfrey have in common?

Each of these individuals discovered what they were good at and dedicated their lives to developing that talent.

You may be an outstanding organizer, an unusually caring individual, a gifted writer, or an extraordinary musician. You each have a special talent that won't necessarily make you famous but, if used to its fullest potential, can help you live a more rewarding life. This lesson will help you identify your most distinguishing talent, skill, or trait—your unique gift.

What is the one thing about you that is unique? There are two sources where you can find answers:

- **What you believe.** When you consider your unique gifts, try to identify the things that, for whatever reason, you do better than anyone else. Take a few minutes right now to answer these questions: What things seem to come naturally to me? What kinds of compliments am I paid? What do I do really well? What am I passionate about? Which accomplishments have made me proud? What brings me the greatest satisfaction?

- **What others say.** Imagine that your family, friends, and co-workers got together in a room and described your greatest talents, abilities, or contributions. What words would they offer?

Which adjectives would they use? You can do the friends-and-family exercise on your own by considering things people have said about you in the past or you can actually ask them to tell you. You can also identify the things for which you've received recognition.

Throughout my life, I have found that positive things happen when you use your greatest gifts. You will develop a stronger sense of self-worth and find more fulfillment in what you do. Perhaps even more important is the enjoyment you gain from what you do and the ripple effect it will have on your entire life.

LTM Challenge

Each one of us has a unique gift that can bring happiness and satisfaction into our lives. Take some quiet time to make a list of your unique gifts. After you make this list, narrow it down to your top ten, then your top five, then to your single most distinguishing quality. Once you have it identified, it's time to start thinking about how you can use it to its full potential.

Don't be discouraged if it takes you a while to figure out how best to use your unique gift. It took me more than a year before I became completely clear on how I would use mine, but it wasn't a year wasted. I learned something every step of the way.

> **If you take the time to discover your unique gift,**
> **you'll unlock the door to**
> **a future of limitless possibilities.**

79. Adopt the Habits of High Performers

To learn how to reach the top in any discipline or job, the smartest thing you can do is study the attributes of those who came before you. What characteristics and traits distinguish them from everyone else? What skills have they mastered? What little things do they do on a regular basis?

When I started my real-estate career at age 23, I flew to Denver to meet with the nation's top-selling Realtor. He was so impressed with my desire to learn that he spent the entire day giving me advice. In the months and years ahead, I implemented his recommendations. Today, as I look back, I firmly believe that his example, encouragement, and counsel contributed greatly to my success as a Realtor.

When I was asked to coach my son's Little League team, I hired two former professional baseball players to coach me. Even though I had played Little League baseball and watched baseball on TV for years, I wanted to learn proper fielding and hitting fundamentals. I learned all I could and with the help of another parent, we coached our team to a 39-1 record over the two years we coached together.

The same strategy was applied to developing *Little Things Matter*. I studied the top ten bloggers on the Internet and sought counsel from those who had expertise in this area. Examining all the LITTLE THINGS that distinguished the top bloggers from all the rest quickly taught me the path to becoming one of the top bloggers in my category.

Here's a top secret. Most successful people are willing to share their wisdom and knowledge. They find it flattering and fulfilling. If you call the top three people in your profession, compliment them on their success, and ask for 30 minutes of their time to help you be the best at what you do, I bet at least one or two would find the time to help you.

LTM Challenge

As you study people at the top in their career fields, make a list of every LITTLE THING they have done and are currently doing to become successful. Your goal is to make a list of 100 LITTLE THINGS. Don't roll your eyes at this number! If you want to be the best, make a list of 100 LITTLE THINGS. Stretch your mind to think of things the average person would not normally notice. Highly successful people didn't get to the top by doing 5, 10 or even 21 things right; they went far beyond their competitors. It won't take you long to realize that every LITTLE THING matters.

Don't just study the habits of one person. Learn from as many as you can. You'll begin to understand what you need to do and you who must become in order to earn the reputation of a top performer in your field.

> **You don't have to reinvent the wheel to be successful.**
> **Rather, learn the activities and model the traits of others**
> **who have already achieved the success you desire.**

80. Learn by Showing Respect and Listening

Communication experts tell us that as much as 85 percent of our learning comes from listening. It follows then that if people take their valuable time to give us instruction or advice, we should concentrate on listening and absorbing the information rather than talking. Sounds simple, right? Perhaps, but in my experience this is easier said than done.

Consider these two illustrations.

1. Harry calls me to kick around some ideas about his new business endeavor. He shares his thought process and asks me what I think. I begin to respond but, within 30 seconds, Harry takes over the conversation, giving me reasons why he made certain decisions. This goes on for the balance of the call. I finally get off the phone frustrated, thinking: *Here's a person who can't shut up and listen without monopolizing the conversation.*

2. George, whom I have never met, sends me an email requesting an appointment to talk about his sales strategy. I agree and block out 30 minutes. During our call George tells me how he approaches his prospective customers and asks my advice on how he can be more effective. As I speak, he listens with great interest and asks a few follow-up questions. I get off the phone with George, finding myself impressed with someone I had never met because he listened intently and asked sensible questions at the appropriate time in the conversation.

Now it's time for true confessions. Recently I sought the advice of someone I respect in the publishing industry. He took time out from his busy schedule to help me make a decision. And what did I find myself doing? Talking too much! Interjecting! I had become one of those people who drive me crazy. I hung up the phone totally disappointed in myself.

I began to interrogate myself, which I always do when I do things I shouldn't have done. Why did I feel the need to interrupt and comment? Did I feel that I needed to agree with his ideas by sharing a related story? Was it ego? Did I feel defensive about the decisions I had made so far? Or was I just excited to share my thoughts with someone I knew to be an expert in the field?

While I am not confident I know the exact answer, I am positive that from this day forward, I am going to *zip it* when people take their time to give me advice and help me grow.

LTM Challenge

How about you? Do you focus completely on what the speaker is saying or do you find yourself talking more than listening when people are giving you advice? From this day forward, when it's time to learn, will you show respect and listen? Are you willing to join me in making this commitment?

> **When it's time to learn, shut up and listen.**

81. Get the Job You Want

You can achieve anything that is important to you if you will focus on the LITTLE THINGS that matter. If you are in the market for a new job, look for the LITTLE THINGS that will give you the edge. No more whining about not being able to get a job! No more complaining about your current job! It's time to push outside of your comfort zone, and do those things that other job applicants are unwilling to do.

I recommend that you take the following steps:

1. **Determine your greatest value.** Assuming you want the highest paying job for your skill set, make a list of your most valuable talents and abilities and rank them based on their value to the market. As an example, if you are an administrative assistant, your skills may range from answering the phone to creating business plans with a salary range from $15/hour to $75/hour. Your job search should then be focused on maximizing your greatest value: writing business plans.

2. **Identify potential positions.** Consider positions that allow you to capitalize on your talents. Using the example above, identify the types of companies and positions within those companies where your primary responsibility would be writing business plans.

3. **Create a targeted résumé.** Once the type of position is identified, create a custom résumé that highlights the specific skill set. Make sure to highlight it in the "job objective" and "previous experience" sections and in the cover letter. Ensure that your résumé presents you in a manner consistent with the wage you are seeking.

4. **Identify potential employers.** Make a list of all the employers who offer the type of position you are seeking. You may have to confine yourself to a specific geographic region, although many employers allow and often encourage employees to work from home. You may even want to consider buying a list of companies that meet your criteria from a list broker. (Type "List broker" in your favorite search engine to identify business list providers.)

5. **Pick up the phone.** Here is where the winners are separated from the complainers. This is the biggest take-away from this lesson: If you want to land the ideal job, you must push yourself outside your comfort zone and call your prospective employers.

The complainers are those who sit at home and look for job postings and allow themselves to compete with 100 other people for the same position. Winners do online research about potential employers; then, using personal initiative, they pick up the phone to make initial contact.

My friends in human resources tell me that very few people proactively call them. People who are in charge of hiring are the very people who appreciate those rare individuals who use their personal initiative. When you do the LITTLE THINGS that impress others, you have the advantage.

When you call a company that is not currently hiring for the position you are seeking, ask if it would be okay to forward your résumé. Then ask for permission to follow up in a couple weeks. If they grant you permission to follow up, they will be more open to accepting your call.

6. **Follow Up.** After you send your résumé with a personalized cover letter, be sure to follow up as appropriate. This will increase the likelihood that your name and résumé will remain at the "top of the pile" when a job opportunity materializes. If you really want to stand out from other applicants, send a handwritten note thanking the person you spoke with for their time and consideration.

LTM Challenge

If you're looking for a new job, do you have the courage to pick up the phone and call prospective employers for as long as it takes to land the job you want? Are you willing to be uncomfortable for a few weeks to get the job that allows you to maximize your gifts and abilities?

If your answer is yes, then I challenge you to do three things:

1. Think outside the box. Be creative and make a list of the LITTLE THINGS you can do to get the edge.

2. Review the tips I have outlined and create a targeted résumé.

3. Once you land an interview, be conscious of your personal brand and do all the LITTLE THINGS to make a positive impression.

> **People who believe in themselves,**
> **aggressively seek what they want,**
> **refuse to accept rejection, and do the LITTLE THINGS**
> **that their competitors are unwilling to do**
> **will be rewarded for their efforts.**

82. Increase Your Value to the Market

A basic foundation of our economic system provides that the amount we earn is based on the value we offer. It follows then that the more value we bring to the market, the more we can charge for our services. Let's probe a little deeper to get a better picture of what this means.

What is the difference between those at the top of the pay scale in a given profession and those at the bottom? Yes, the people at the top of the pay scale receive a higher salary because of their skills, but there's an intangible here that is often missed. People at the top of the pay scale are recognized and rewarded for all the LITTLE THINGS they do to bring value to the organization.

If you want to earn more money, you must first increase your value. Only after increasing your value can you expect to charge more for your services. It doesn't work like many people think: Pay me more and I will do more. That is the mindset of a low-wage employee who never gets ahead. The entrepreneurial-minded employee sounds something like this: Let me do all I can to increase my value and if my current employer doesn't value that, then I will market my services to another employer.

New Way of Thinking

My oldest son Gerrid's first job as a bagger at a local grocery store is a good example. His employer's instructions were simple enough: ask the customers if they want paper or plastic; as you pack the groceries in the bags, put like items together and don't make the bags too heavy. One day Gerrid came home discouraged. He said, "*Dad, this job is not at all challenging; it's meaningless.*"

Gerrid's dismay was a perfect opportunity for me to share my *little-things-matter* philosophy and to help him understand how he could improve his value and self-image. I reminded him that—although he wouldn't earn any additional money because the salary of a bagger was limited—it was important for him to perform the role of a bagger in the best possible way.

I encouraged him to look at this job as an opportunity to grow, to become a better person, and to prepare for the future. I challenged him to think of ways to go beyond his employer's normal expectations: keeping his shoes shined and clothes pressed, smiling at the customers, offering them a friendly greeting, making eye contact, thanking them for their business, and volunteering to do the things the other employees did not want to do.

My goal was to teach Gerrid a new way of thinking—to focus on the LITTLE THINGS he could do to increase his value to the marketplace. It wasn't long before he began to enjoy his work, winning the appreciation and admiration of his employer and co-workers. This life lesson stayed with Gerrid throughout his teens and early 20s. Today, at age 24, he owns a highly successful business and is the first person I go to for business advice.

Compounding Effect

Focusing on the LITTLE THINGS to enhance your value will add up. Going the extra mile brings great rewards because so few people make this effort. As you make small changes, you will see an increase in your value. At first it may not be measurable, but your ultimate success will come as a result of a compounding effect of doing the LITTLE THINGS over a long period of time. It comes from making small improvements day after day, week after week, month after month, and year after year.

Compare your success to investing your money. Just as interest compounds over time, so will your value if you stretch yourself to build your value each day.

LTM Challenge

What's your current value to the market? Seriously! How much are you worth? If you were a publicly traded company, what would be the price of your stock? How much would you buy?

As you look to increase your value, focus on two things.

- First, be intentional about performing your core job description at the highest level of excellence you are capable of achieving.

- Second, be conscious about doing those things that go above and beyond your job description. It's all the things you do without having to be asked that will distinguish you from your peers.

> **The most significant increase in your value
> will be achieved if you know
> the LITTLE THINGS that matter
> and do them consistently
> at your highest level of excellence.**

83. Think Like an Entrepreneur

Some of us market our services to our employers; some of us market our services directly to consumers. Regardless of who buys our personal services, we are the owners of our businesses, and we market our services for a fee. In essence, we are all entrepreneurs and should adopt an entrepreneurial mindset.

One of the few times when employees actually view themselves as entrepreneurs is when they market themselves to prospective employers. They put together an impressive résumé and market their services. They put on their best behavior during the interview process as they describe their services with confidence. Once hired, they go back to thinking like an employee. It's time to change that way of thinking.

Who's in charge of your income and career? If you believe your employer is in charge, then you will find yourself continuing to be a victim of circumstances outside your control. On the other hand, if you view yourself as someone in control of your career, you will feel like you are also in control of your life. As goes one's career, so goes one's life.

Follow in the Footsteps of an Entrepreneur

- Entrepreneurs view themselves as people who control their destinies. When you believe you are in control of the Number 1 thing you do in life, you feel the power of being in control of everything you do.

- Entrepreneurs know what needs to be done and they do it without direction or supervision from others. This is a challenge for most people because we all have been programmed to take instructions from others. It began in childhood as our parents and teachers told us what to do and it continued with the traditional employer–employee relationship.

- Entrepreneurs are accountable to themselves for their actions and decisions. They know that their success comes from doing what needs to be done to satisfy their clients or customers. While there may be many things they prefer not to do, their personal initiative is an overriding characteristic and driving force.

- Entrepreneurs know their value to the market is based on their personal brand and the quality and type of the services they provide. They always look for the refinements they can make to create more value and enhance their brand.

- Entrepreneurs recognize that income follows value. They know that before they can expect to increase their profits, they must first increase the value of their services.

- Entrepreneurs nurture their relationships with their customers, knowing that people do business with people they like and trust.

Tips for Developing an Entrepreneurial Mindset

1. If you are marketing your servicers to an employer, start to treat your employer like your most important customer. Build your relationship with your customer (employer) and your customer's employees (co-workers).

Do more than you are expected to do with a positive attitude. Do the little things that make your employer want to do business with you!

2. Perform your responsibilities with excellence and never require anyone to remind you of your responsibilities or hold you accountable. Take pride in always doing what is expected of you.

3. Always project a positive business image from the way you dress to the way you conduct yourself. Remember, you are an entrepreneur and your brand influences your market value.

4. If you work for an employer who does not place the same value on your services as you do, perhaps it's time to look in the mirror and make a realistic assessment of your services. If you feel they are not appreciated, perhaps it's time find a different employer (customer).

LTM Challenge

Awareness is where all change begins. Since we are all entrepreneurs, start thinking of yourself as a business owner and your services as your product. When you adopt the mindset of an entrepreneur, you will feel a rush of adrenaline as you begin to see that you really are in control of your income and career. If you are an employee, you will quickly become every employer's dream.

> **You have everything to gain by starting to think like an entrepreneur and nothing to lose.**

84. Be Smart About the Risks You Take

Risks are a part of living. Not every day, but certainly periodically. I'm referring to risks where there's a lack of complete certainty and where several possible outcomes could exist—at least one of which is undesirable. Sounds dangerous with a negative connotation, right? Not necessarily. The right risks at the right time can be very positive. It comes down to developing a practical framework for wise decision-making when risk is a factor. For example:

- Leaving a secure position with an established company to accept a more lucrative job with a new start-up. Possible outcome: What if the business fails?

- Entering into a partnership with a new business associate. Possible outcome: What if the person turns out to have different values than you have—values that cannot be reconciled?

- Investing a large sum of money in a new investment opportunity. Possible outcome: What if it fails and you lose it all?

Sadly, the evidence of bad risks and the decisions that follow are all too common. I have had friends who were millionaires but lost it all as a result of taking unnecessary risks. I also had a friend lose his life in a deep-water scuba diving accident. In his quest for the thrill, he risked it all, leaving behind a widow with two teenage daughters.

If you desire to live a successful, fulfilling life and retire with enough money to enjoy your retirement, you must take calculated risks. This includes risks in relationships, in your career, and in your investments.

While taking smart calculated risks is vital to reaching your goals in life, taking poor risks and losing can set you back, sometimes significantly. Remember that taking smart risks is as simple as making wise decisions.

I've learned a lot in my life about risk taking from observing others and through my personal experiences—both good and bad. Now when I consider taking a risk, I ask myself six questions:

1. **What are the risks?** Don't let your enthusiasm prevent you from carefully considering all possible risks. Your greatest risk may be overlooking what is at stake.

2. **What are the odds of one of the risks being realized?** Use data whenever you can by doing research. Talk to others who have been in similar circumstances.

3. **What are the rewards?** Be realistic as you evaluate the offer. Can you really quit your day job and devote ten hours a week to something and make $100,000 a year? (Probably not.)

4. **What are the odds of those rewards?** Once again, find out about others who have done something similar and how they have fared.

5. **What other options do you have?** Do your homework; don't limit yourself. Buying that investment property is not your only investment option.

6. **Do I need to make this decision today?** Remember the old adage: *Fools rush in where angels fear to tread.* Take the time you need to do your research and explore your options.

After you answer these six questions, remove all emotion from your decision and ask yourself what your gut is telling you. Also, never forget about the wild card risk—you don't know what you don't know!

LTM Challenge

The next time you find yourself faced with a decision involving an element of risk, I urge you to review this lesson and keep the following three things in mind:

- **Start small.** You don't need to hit a grand slam your first time at bat. Aim for singles and only advance to the next base when you feel like the odds are in your favor. You can live an amazing life, travel the world, and retire financially secure if you just keep hitting singles.

- **Don't get greedy.** This is a potential problem in any area, but especially in the financial realm. Some people never accumulate wealth because they spend most of their money in risky ventures. Others save money for years and then get tired of working, roll the dice with their savings hoping to strike it big, and end up losing it all.

- **Approach partnerships with caution.** One of the ways to reduce risks is by not giving up control. For a partnership to work, it must begin with a well-established relationship.

> **Taking smart calculated risks is as simple as making wise and unemotional decisions.**

85. Take Control of Your Finances

How would you like to be in command of your finances—never be in debt again, live free of financial pressure, and retire comfortably when that day arrives? This is possible, but it will require you do three crucial things: put together a budget, track your expenses, and commit to spending less than you earn.

If you want to lead a financially responsible life, then you must have a personal or household budget. Here are a few reasons for living by a budget:

- Control how your money is spent, saved, and invested
- Plan for future expenses
- Understand exactly where your money is going
- Know what you can and cannot afford
- Live within your means and stay out of debt.

Have you ever found yourself at the end of a month wondering where all the money went? While it's easy to look back and identify the big expenses, it's the little ones that add up both in the short term and long term.

As an example, spending $4 a day on a cup of coffee adds up to $120 a month or $1,440 a year. If, instead of spending it on coffee, you choose to invest the $4 a day at 8 percent interest, your gain would be $51,833.79 at the end of 20 years. Making your own lunches rather than eating out could also achieve a similar result. You save an extra $100,000—if you do both.

When you create a budget and start tracking expenses, you'll no longer have to wonder where your money went; you will know. Take control by making informed and unemotional decisions *in advance* about how to spend your money.

There are a number of online resources and at your local public library that make it easy to start and maintain a budget. Simply type *"how to make a budget"* in your favorite search engine for step-by-step directions, free templates, budget calculators, and tips for sticking to a budget.

Putting together a budget is not complicated or difficult. Here are the key components of any household budget:

- Monthly income (include all sources: paychecks, disability payments, etc.)

- Mandatory or fixed expenses (mortgage or rent, car payments, insurance, child care, etc.)

- Discretionary or controllable expenses (entertainment, dining out, vacations, groceries, utilities, hobbies, etc.)

- Charitable giving (church and other non-profit agencies)

- Future needs (savings, emergencies, college funds, retirement)

How much money you allocate to each category will be largely based on your income. Many people use the 10/10/80 guide: 10 percent of your income goes toward savings and planning for the future, 10 percent goes toward charitable giving, and the remaining 80 percent goes toward your mandatory and discretionary expenses.

If you find there is not enough money to distribute according to that formula, decide what you must and are willing to change. For example, can you reduce your mandatory or fixed monthly expenses by downsizing or refinancing? Are there discretionary items you can eliminate from your budget? These are personal decisions that only you can make.

LTM Challenge

When it comes to budgeting and managing personal finances, there's room for improvement in all of us. If you don't already have a budget, I strongly encourage you to set one up and start tracking your expenses this month. Use your budget to get smart about your hard-earned money and take control of your financial future.

> **The day you set up a budget**
> **and start tracking your expenses is**
> **the day you take control of your financial future.**

86. Organize Your Day With a To-Do List

Everyone who knows me well also knows about my white pad that goes everywhere I go. This is my To-Do List—my prioritized daily action plan I use to increase productivity, reduce stress, and keep me focused. Of the more than 100 time management rules I follow, using a prioritized daily To-Do List does more to increase my productivity than any other. It removes the guesswork about how I spend my time and with whom I spend it.

Here's the routine. Before you go to bed, take out a pad of paper and write down everything you need to get done. As you make your list, don't focus on prioritizing it. Just drain your brain and make your list as long as it needs to be, including everything you can think of that needs your attention. Researchers tell us that when you know your plan for the next day, your mind works on it during the night while you are sleeping.

Once the list is complete, you are ready to categorize your tasks.

- Put an "A" next to things that *absolutely must get done first.* These are the things that will bring you closer to the accomplishment of your most important goals.

- Put a "B" next to activities that *you should get done.* An example might be paying bills, or getting your dirty car washed.

- Put a "C" next to those things *you need to do but just aren't a priority today.* An example is picking up the dry cleaning that you don't need for a couple days.

- Finally, put a "D" next to *things you can delegate.* This might be something you ask your spouse or children to do such as mailing a package or running an errand.

  After you have categorized all the items on your list with an A, B, C or D, you are ready to prioritize them.

- Review all the "A" items and write a 1 next to the most important A; a 2 next to the second most important A; a 3 next to the third most important A, and so on until you are done with all of your A items.

- Then go over your "B" items. Write a 1 next to your most important B, and follow the same procedure as you did with your A's until all your B's are prioritized.

- You don't need to prioritize your "C" items now because you seldom have time to get to them until they move up in importance. However, do keep them on the list so you won't forget about them.

- Review the "D" items and delegate them to the appropriate people.

Once your list is complete, you'll have a prioritized plan for the next day. You'll go to bed and rest comfortably—feeling organized, less stressed, and focused on tackling A-1 first thing the next morning. A word of caution! Don't be tempted to look down the list for the easy things you could do quickly. Not only would that defeat the purpose of having a prioritized To-Do List, but it would also give you a false sense of accomplishment.

During the years that I was aggressively expanding my businesses, I made it a point to do my prospecting first thing in the morning because this was the most important activity I could engage in to achieve my goals. The morning was also the time of day when most people were in a good mood and receptive to my calls. Every day my list started with "A-1

Prospecting." As I write this book, my A-1 activity every day is writing these lessons—not only because of its importance in completing my goal but also because morning is my most creative period of the day.

LTM Challenge

Make a prioritized To-Do List each day for the next week and see how it affects the way you spend your time and what you accomplish. Notice how your stress level decreases and your sense of self-satisfaction increases. Start the day focused with one thing on your mind: A-1.

> **Keeping and acting on a prioritized daily To-Do List
> increases your productivity, reduces stress,
> and makes you more responsible.**

87. Batch Your Tasks

Effective time management is essential if you want to achieve your career goals, balance your career and family, or manage your household.

Batching your tasks entails combining similar responsibilities into one category and performing them at the same time. Examples include running all your errands at one time rather than throughout the day, or going to the grocery store once a week rather than twice a week.

Often it's the little tasks that steal our time. For instance, have you ever thought about what it takes to pay bills—one at a time? Instead of paying them one at a time, we can increase our productivity by paying them in batches. For 20 years I paid bills twice a month, each time taking me about two hours. In an effort to further improve my productivity, I recently switched to paying them only on the 25th of the month. It now takes me three hours to pay all my monthly bills and complete the related accounting. This refinement saves me one hour every month.

Another valuable benefit of batching your tasks is that the quality of your work will improve and errors will be reduced. As a sales professional, I always blocked out windows of time to make my sales calls. This not only forced me to do what I didn't want to do, but after a couple of calls I found my rhythm and my results improved.

Task-Batching Ideas

- **Return emails**. Set your rule and stick with it. Two or three times a day works for me. You may have to scan emails in between projects in case something requires your immediate attention, but remain disciplined to batch your email correspondence.

- **Open mail.** When I go through my daily mail, I throw all magazines, junk mail, and anything without a first-class stamp into our recycling container. I immediately read personal mail, and put all bills into a box and only open them once a month at bill-paying time.

- **Social media.** Establish reasonable rules of engagement for yourself because Facebook, Twitter, LinkedIn, and other social media platforms can be addicting and huge time wasters.

- **Scheduled phone calls.** I schedule all my calls in the afternoon back-to-back rather than scattering them throughout the afternoon. This gives me a reason to conclude the call and I find that if people know there is specific allotted time to the call, they are more likely to get right to the point.

LTM Challenge

Is batching your tasks something you currently do as you plan each day? If not, start combining your responsibilities into categories and do them at the same time. You'll be amazed at the power of this one time management tip. If you currently batch your tasks, identify the refinements you can make to increase your productivity.

> **If you make batching your tasks
> part of your daily routine,
> you will increase your productivity
> and perform at a higher level.**

88. Control Interruptions

One of the basic fundamentals of time management is to focus on one thing at a time. I read an article recently that said every time you allow an interruption you lose ten minutes of productivity. If you are interrupted while working on a task or project, that interruption is more than just a distraction; it requires you to take additional time to gather your thoughts and return to your original state of focus before the interruption occurred.

The most common source of interruptions comes from family, friends, and co-workers. All these people are important. However, if you don't establish boundaries, you can be assured people will feel comfortable interrupting you on their whim.

Tips to help you control interruptions

- **Turn off all notifications on your cell phone device.** While I value the importance of providing a high level of service, I also know that I don't need to drop what I'm doing and disrupt my thought process every time someone calls or sends me a text. If you are in the midst of an important project and don't want to be distracted, consider turning off your cell phone. You can return messages during breaks between tasks or during windows of time you allocate for such responsibilities.

- **Turn off all distractions on your computer.** This includes your email, instant messaging, and social media notifications. Instead, block out time to return emails and visit your social media sites. I check emails two or three times a day and engage in social networking one or two times a day.

- **Don't accept unscheduled phone calls.** Of course emergencies are an exception. As a general rule, I don't accept unscheduled calls. When I schedule my days, I block out time to complete each project. If I allow myself to accept unscheduled calls, it's unlikely that I can complete my projects on time. If I get an unscheduled call while I am in the middle of something, I generally look at the number and, unless I feel I must answer the phone, I don't. Then when I am in between projects, I check messages and return calls.

- **Set boundaries on workplace interruptions.** If you work in an environment where you are constantly being interrupted, start to log all the interruptions. As you do, make a note next to the ones that were urgent and needed your immediate attention. I think you will be shocked with your results. Once you evaluate your results, consider establishing boundaries to reduce your interruptions.

LTM Challenge

I realize that, as is the case with any time-management technique, there will always be exceptions; controlling interruptions is no different. Your first step is to recognize that you don't need to be available every time someone wants to reach you. Your next step is to take control of how you spend your time rather than allowing other people and circumstances to control it.

For all my time management tips, download the free report under the REPORTS tab at LittleThingsMatter.com.

> **You can't be productive**
> **when you are constantly being interrupted.**

89. Find Balance Between Work and Family

Although I haven't been the perfect husband or father, I have always been a great believer in leading a balanced life. I take pride in being a successful entrepreneur as well as a devoted family man. Married to my high-school sweetheart for 25 years, we have raised and home-schooled four remarkable children, ranging in age from 15–24.

I realize there are elements to living a happy and successful life beyond family and career, but finding the right balance between these two is where many people struggle. For those of you who are high achievers, it is absolutely critical that you maintain an appropriate balance in your life. If you neglect to invest time in relationships with your spouse and children, you will likely experience serious regrets in the future.

For those of you who are spouses of high achievers, accept the fact that 40 hours a week is *break even* in life. If you want to enjoy a better-than-average quality of life, there are sacrifices you must make. If you aren't making these compromises, beware. I have never seen a marriage last when someone's spouse is holding him or her back. Have you?

Ten Tips for Enjoying a Balanced Life

1. **Set your family and career goals.** Most of you are familiar with setting personal goals. Equally important is the identification of your family goals. If you have not done so, write down your goals for three separate categories: your career, marriage, and family.

2. **Get support from your spouse.** The only way you are going to achieve these goals is with the support of your spouse. Just as it would be unwise to think you can build a successful business

244. LITTLE THINGS MATTER

without the support of your business partner, you won't build a successful marriage, family life, or career without the support of your spouse.

3. **Create blocks of time for work and family.** One of the first things my wife and I did when we got married was to put together a work and family schedule. What started out 25 years ago as a simple schedule where we blocked out time for my work and time for us to be together has transitioned to a plan for our entire family. We designate blocks of time to spend with each child and together as a family. This one tip has made an incredible difference in my life and in the lives of my children.

4. **Review the schedule with family.** After you and your spouse have negotiated these blocks of time, review the schedule with your children and get their buy-in.

5. **Make sure your work time is respected.** If you are self-employed make sure everyone respects your work schedule by not interrupting you unless it's something that cannot wait.

6. **Don't conduct business during family time.** It's important that during family time, you focus on your family. When I'm with my family, I don't schedule calls or appointments. I don't check my email or go into my office to finish a project. My phone seldom rings during family time because everyone who knows me well respects those boundaries.

7. **Protect your family time.** No texts, no emails, no phone calls! This applies to every family member. Make your family time a sacred time that is valued by everyone.

8. **Be present.** Focus on your family. Put aside thoughts of other people or activities. Resist the temptation to talk about your work; instead, concentrate on topics of interest to your family. Use this time to ask questions and discuss what is going on in their lives.

9. **Spend time with each child separately.** If you have children, let me encourage you to block out time to spend with each one on an individual basis. There is no better way to connect with someone than one-to-one. Whether it's a bike ride, an overnight camping trip, a game of checkers, a cup of tea, or whatever it is they enjoy doing. Block out time each week to spend with each child.

10. **Plan a weekly date with your spouse.** This is the Number 1 marriage tip I give to newlyweds. Every week for the past 25 years (with rare exception) my wife and I have a date. Our dates may be dinner at our favorite restaurant, a boat ride, or a campfire on the beach cooking hot dogs. The key for us is *getting out of the house* where we can focus on each other without any distractions.

LTM Challenge

It's time for self-evaluation. Are you leading a balanced life or are things out of whack? Is your career dominating? I challenge you to take whatever steps are necessary to improve the balance between the time spent pursuing your career, building your marriage, and pouring love into your children's lives.

> **Focusing on your family and spending time
> with each member is the foundation for a healthy marriage,
> a happy home, and a satisfying career.**

90. Stressed to the Max?

Do you sometimes feel like a superhero? Juggling a full-time job with carpooling and housework, volunteering at your church fundraiser, caring for an aging parent, and the list goes on. Your To-Do List keeps growing. Just as one thing gets dealt with, another one comes up and then another. Before you know it, you are overwhelmed. You felt as calm as the ocean foam gently lapping against the rocks until it suddenly turned into a tidal wave submerging everything in its path.

A small amount of stress can be a healthy motivator; however, higher amounts can cause you to be irritable, depressed, and susceptible to illness. I have done a number of things over the years that have helped prevent me from being overwhelmed, such as developing good time management skills, controlling my commitments, setting proper expectations, and finding the right balance between work, play, and family. However, there are still times when I find myself overwhelmed.

Seven Steps to Take When Feeling Overwhelmed

Step 1. **List all responsibilities.** When the work looks insurmountable and you find it hard to breathe, stop everything and take 30 minutes to review and prioritize your responsibilities.

Step 2. **Strategize.** Assess what is involved in completing each of these responsibilities to fully understand what needs to be accomplished and the amount of time it will take.

Step 3. **Create two lists.** When you have a clear understanding of what needs to get done, create two lists. This first list includes the things only you can do, listed in priority order. The second list contains the items you can delegate to others, also in a prioritized sequence.

Step 4. **Delegate.** Whether you are an employer, employee, a spouse, or a student, delegating can lighten your load. Who can you call on when you are in a crunch? Who could type your report or do your research? Would a friend or neighbor be willing to pick up your children from soccer practice? Could your kids help you by making copies or preparing dinner?

When you get caught up with your work, do something to express your appreciation to those who helped you. As long as you bring value to your relationships, people will be happy to help you.

Step 5. **Take Responsibility.** Now it's time to evaluate the things that only you can do. Determine if there are enough hours in a day to complete these tasks on time. I am not talking about normal working hours. I mean all available hours outside of sleeping and eating. Since I take great pride in being a person who is responsible, I will get up an hour earlier, stay up an hour later, or work weekends to fulfill my responsibilities.

If you determine that you can't complete something on time, immediately call the people who will be affected. Without making excuses, explain the situation and tell them when you anticipate the project will be completed. No one likes to hear about a missed deadline, but everyone appreciates having the advance notice.

Step 6. Attack. Turn off the phone, shut down your email, and attack your responsibilities in priority sequence. Every big thing is made up of little things so just do them in priority sequence.

Sometimes you may feel like you are walking in quicksand, but just keep trudging and eventually it all gets done. When you attack your responsibilities in a prioritized sequence, you feel less stressed because you will know you are working your plan and doing all you can do.

Step 7. Learn. After you get caught up, evaluate those stressful periods to learn from your experiences. Here's what I have learned:

- Don't over commit; learn when to say no.
- Manage expectations.
- Don't agree to deadlines unless you can fulfill your responsibilities on time with excellence.
- Don't procrastinate by waiting until the last minute to do something.

LTM Challenge

Bend the corner of this page. When you find yourself overwhelmed with tasks and responsibilities, remember to review this lesson and incorporate all six steps to manage your stress and fulfill your responsibilities.

> **When you feel overwhelmed, don't give up.**
> **By organizing, strategizing, delegating,**
> **and attacking, you can shake off**
> **the stress and anxiety that is holding you down.**

91. Enjoy Life's Journey

The popular quote by Ralph Waldo Emerson—*"Life is a journey, not a destination"*—can be found on posters and bumper stickers. It's been paraphrased and used to train sales teams, give advice to college graduates, and counsel our over-scheduled friends.

As is the case with any overused expression or phrase, we tend to overlook its significance and dismiss the message entirely. Nevertheless, I believe the subject bears some serious consideration.

Far too often we spend our time in hot pursuit of our goals and don't take the time to enjoy the people and experiences along the way. Everyone seems to be in a hurry to get something, always focusing on what they want rather than appreciating what they have.

As I pondered my own success-driven life, I've often felt like I was running a race rather than enjoying the ride. I suspect all high achievers have a similar perspective. Here's my advice. Don't wait for the funeral of a loved one to recognize how fleeting life can be. Don't wish you had more time to spend with your spouse, children, or friends. Don't miss out on all that life has to offer in your pursuit to be successful.

If you want to enjoy life, take time out—notice the deep purple of the violets and the orange-pink sky of the sunset. Listen to the morning symphony of the birds, laugh at a child's antics, relish a hotdog at a ball game, let your body and mind relax, and spend more time with treasured friends and family.

I have made a list of things to help me find pleasure in the balance of my journey. I would encourage you to do the same.

- I am going to concentrate on having more fun. I will smile and laugh. I will tell jokes. I will go fishing frequently and play golf more often.

- I will continue to place a priority on spending time with family and friends, enjoying the activities that we can do together.

- I want to enjoy nature—a walk in the park or on the beach, the birds chirping, the flowers blooming, and the waves rolling along the shore.

- I will control my reactions and appreciate other people's differences. I do not have to win all the battles. I am not going to allow myself to get worked up over things that really don't matter in the big scope of life.

- I will block out time to recharge my batteries. As an entrepreneur, it's easy to work 24/7.

- I will be happy with where I am at any given time and give my full attention to the people I am with at the time.

- I will eagerly and optimistically anticipate the thrill of the next great challenge or adventure.

LTM Challenge

I hope my personal introspection gives you some ideas. What will you do differently to find more pleasure and contentment along your journey? Don't get to the end of your life and wish you had made other choices that could have brought you more joy. Start today to seek a better way!

> **Embrace life as a wonderful adventure
> and enjoy every moment to its fullest.**

92. Lead During Difficult Times

It's easy to lead during the best of times; however, it's the tough times that really breed and define great leaders. Look around. How many people do you see who are stepping up their games and navigating challenging circumstances? As I write this book, we are in the midst of a leadership drought. The economic downturn has exposed everyone's warts. It has separated bona fide leaders from those who thought they were leaders.

Each of us has an opportunity to lead, to take control of our own lives, and to build our future. Whether you lead a business, department, team, nonprofit organization, religious institution, or family, here are some thoughts for you to consider on being an extraordinary leader during tough and challenging times.

1. **Seize the moment.** Today's leaders realize that <u>now</u> is the time to distinguish themselves. Knowing that most people don't have what it takes to lead during difficult times, true leaders are growing, pushing, and stretching like never before. While their progress may be slow due to negative economic currents, they are gaining ground and separating themselves from those who are slipping back.

2. **Focus on offense.** In challenging times staunch leaders aren't griping and complaining like those who seem to have crawled into their defensive cocoons. Instead, they have *sucked it up*, learned their lessons, and are focused on offense.

3. **Become a student of successful predecessors.** Great leaders aren't born; they are sculpted through years of learning and growth. They understand the only way to improve is through learning. Today's leaders are hungry for knowledge that will inspire, motivate, and give them the edge. They also know the best source of valuable content comes from their successful predecessors.

4. **Put together your plan.** Tough times make it all the more necessary for developing a working plan. This is not a time for a wing and a prayer. Extraordinary leaders carefully choose their target and map out the path that will take them successfully to the achievement of their goal.

5. **Fight to win.** It's easy to get discouraged and have moments of doubt and fear when faced with challenging and difficult times. Wise leaders often get down, but rather than wallowing in self-

pity, tenacious leaders are kicking, scratching, and fighting to win. They know deep inside their gut that <u>now</u> is the time to attack.

6. **Position yourself.** The leaders of the future are like farmers, working hard to plant their crops, knowing full well that you must sow before you reap. When the season changes, the harvest will come and they will be positioned to lead like never before.

LTM Challenge

No matter who you are or where you are, I challenge you to step it up. Grab hold of the reins and become a role model. Our world is starving for committed leaders who will be the example for others to follow.

If you have never been a leader, start looking for opportunities where you can fill a leadership role. As your confidence grows, take on bigger projects. It could be a little scary at first, but keep in mind that all great leaders started leading small projects; as their confidence and knowledge grew, they took on larger projects with each one building on the previous.

If you want to control your future, then become a leader of the future. It's the leaders who have control, not the followers. As you seize leadership opportunities you'll begin to distinguish yourself from 95 percent of your peers. The process of inspiring and motivating others will enhance your self-worth, your market value, and your contribution to society.

> **It's piloting through the valley of fear, darkness, and doubt that defines great leaders.**

93. The Duplication Effect of Leadership

Whether or not you hold the formal title of "leader," there are people around you who are influenced by the things you do and don't do. It may be your spouse, children, friends, co-workers, or students. The fact is that you are leading people whether you realize it or not and, by the end of this lesson, you'll see that your role in leading others is much more significant than you may think.

Look for the common thread in these illustrations:

The first one is taken from history.

> Alexander the Great, King of Macedonia, was one of the most outstanding leaders of all time. He became king at the age of 19 and for the next 11 years, he conquered much of the known world, leading his armies against others far superior to his. Yet, when he was at the height of his power, he would still draw his sword at the beginning of a battle and lead his men forward into the conflict. King Alexander felt that he could not ask his men to risk their lives unless he was willing to demonstrate by his actions that he had complete confidence in the outcome. Seeing their leader charge forward motivated his soldiers so that nothing could stop them.
>
> Not only did he lead his men, but also through his example, he taught them how to lead.

Here is a realistic scenario from the business world.

Imagine a company where employees are expected to be at their desks by 8 a.m., yet their manager often strolls in around 8:15 a.m. It doesn't take long for the staff to follow suit, regardless of the official start time.

Contrast that with the manager who requests that his employees stay late to meet a deadline and he is the last one to turn out the lights.

The third illustration is from our personal lives.

Johnny is a member of the Little League baseball team. Johnny's father is the coach. Johnny comes up to bat and hits a grounder to the shortstop and runs as fast as he can towards first base. He is sure he is safe, but the umpire calls him out. Johnny's father storms out and hollers at the umpire.

In the next inning, a teammate strikes out on what he believes is a bad call, so he does the same thing he saw his coach do. He argues with the umpire.

It's critical to recognize that when you lead by example, in a positive or negative way, the impact of your leadership increases exponentially. Each little thing you do leaves footprints for those who follow your example. What you do as a leader not only impacts those you lead but, through your example, you are teaching others how to lead. This duplication effect can influence every person who falls directly or indirectly under your leadership, and it can continue for future generations.

Other leadership qualities are vital, but none compare to the example we set. This holds true in marriage, in parenting, and in the workplace. It applies to everything you do—from being a good listener, responding positively to problems, conducting yourself professionally in meetings, to greeting people cordially in public.

Excellence starts at the top! Families, community groups, and corporations all take on the characteristics of their leaders. When leaders set high performance standards for themselves, others strive to do the same. Therefore, if you want the people around you to step up their game, you must do it first.

We will do well to remember the words of Albert Einstein: *"Setting an example is not the main means of influencing another, it is the only means."*

LTM Challenge

Here are a few tips to help you remember the importance of leading by example:

- The next time you are faced with a decision, ask yourself: *"What would I want my people doing if they were faced with this same situation?"* Your answer will tell you which direction you should go.

- As you work on your own personal and professional development, make a point of sharing what you learn with the people in your circle of influence. Many times we can use our mistakes as humbling examples to teach others. Help them discover the little things they can do to perform at a higher level.

- The next time you need to counsel someone who made an error, look for any connections that may exist between their misstep and your leadership.

> **Every LITTLE THING you do to get better**
> **will help the people you lead get better.**
> **If you want those you lead to improve,**
> **you must improve first.**

94. Become a Respected Rival

Competition is all around us. It arises whenever two or more parties strive for a goal that cannot be shared. Perhaps it's a heated game of Monopoly, a high-stakes sales competition, or an intense tennis match.

I'd like to present ten traits of great competitors. Applicable in any competitive situation, adopting these traits will help you become a respected rival. Reflect on your behavior as you read this lesson. Which have you mastered? In which areas do you need to improve?

1. **Congratulate your opponents when they win or experience success.** This is the first rule of good sportsmanship and is equally applicable in the workplace. When your opponent has done something well, such as making a good shot in tennis or golf, congratulate them. If you lose a competition, extending

congratulations with sincerity demonstrates that you are not a bitter loser and lets your opponent know you won't harbor ill feelings.

2. **Be a gracious winner**. Never rub a loss in your opponent's face. No one likes to be around people who gloat over their wins.

3. **Celebrate respectfully**. It's normal to feel good after a win and want to celebrate, but be conscious of others who may not share in your jubilation. Excessive celebration is a turnoff to most people.

4. **Maintain a sense of decorum**. Always be mindful not to say derogatory things about your competitor, their team, or their candidate. Remember that when you speak poorly of your competitors, it damages your credibility and reputation in the process.

5. **Don't be a sore loser.** Some people pout and display a negative attitude when they lose. How do you feel about those people? Do you want to compete with them again? When you lose a competition, it is normal to feel dejected, but don't get labeled a sore loser.

6. **Use restraint**. If you're on a team, play your part or your position; don't try to cover for anyone else. If it's an individual contest, do your best, but also use your opponent's level of ability as a guide for how intense your participation should be.

7. **Keep a lid on your frustration**. If you must rely on others to win a competition and find yourself frustrated with their poor performance, try not to let it show. Your visible frustration only discourages your teammates and makes you appear arrogant and self-centered. Instead, be the voice of encouragement.

8. **Play fair.** You lose all credibility as a worthy competitor when you cheat. Even worse, you will lose people's respect.

9. **Give the advantage to your opponent.** When a play or other measure of performance is questionable, give your opponent the benefit of the doubt. Rarely will this cost you the competition and it will always reflect well on your character.

10. **Avoid complaining or making excuses**. We have all heard things like, *"I couldn't see the ball because the sun was in my eyes,"* or *"I've had so much going on in my life I just couldn't seem to focus."* No matter how you disguise it, when you complain or make excuses, it is perceived as whining. Nobody enjoys being around a whiner.

If you are as much of a competitor as I am, some of these pointers will require self-control and some serious self-talk. I must admit that I learned a lot of this the hard way, but I have yet to participate in a friendly competition where winning was more important than my reputation or my relationship with my competitors.

LTM Challenge

The next time you find yourself in the middle of a friendly competition, focus on being the kind of competitor people enjoy playing against.

> **Long after the competition is over,
> what will matter the most is not whether you won or lost,
> but how you played the game.**

95. A Simple Life Is a Better Life

What are some of the things you enjoy most in life? What do you value most? I'm guessing that making repairs, paying bills, managing investments, shopping for insurance, or filing paperwork aren't anywhere near the top of your list. If you're like me, they don't even make the cut. I like the simple things like spending time with my family and friends—going for long walks on the beautiful beaches of the Gulf of Mexico and relaxing in the majestic, serene Rocky Mountains where there's no phone or Internet service.

This lesson is about recognizing the advantages that a simple life has to offer. I truly believe that a simple life is about making decisions that result in your ability to spend more time doing the things you enjoy—the activities that bring you happiness and fulfillment.

Over the years, I have learned that it is the accumulation of things that prevents us from doing what we enjoy. I know this having lived both kinds of lifestyles: one of material affluence and the other, a simpler, unencumbered life. I can tell you with certainty that a simple life is a better life.

From the earliest days, my goal was to make enough money so that I could invest wisely, retire early, and have plenty of time to devote to the things that bring me the most joy. Ironically, I ended up getting trapped (temporarily) by the very things I purchased.

As most people do when they achieve a certain level of financial success, I made a list of things to purchase, including a dream home, new cars, and a boat. I succumbed to the false notion that having bigger and better things—jet skis, motorcycles, multiple real estate properties—would lead to more happiness. Over time I discovered that when I accumulated more than I needed, I paid a much higher price for these things in terms of time, worry, frustration, and emotional energy.

Now I think twice before buying anything that has the potential to add complexity to my life. We live in a comfortable home that meets our needs. It's easier and less expensive to maintain than any of our previous homes. Now rather than buying things that are going to add complexity to our lives, we rent what we want and don't worry about a thing.

LTM Challenge

Before spending money, ask yourself:

- Do I really need to own this?
- Will this purchase add more complexity to my life?
- How much time will I have to invest in this purchase?
- Does this purchase come with any hidden emotional energy investment that I may regret later?

More often than not, you will find that the purchases you're considering will cost you much more than the price tag leads you to believe. As your income and success grow, I encourage you to keep things simple and put an emphasis on saving and giving, not spending.

> **Happiness doesn't come from the accumulation of things.**
> **It comes from being satisfied with who you are**
> **and the pleasure you get from**
> **the relationships and quality of life you enjoy.**

262. LITTLE THINGS MATTER

96. Don't Wish You Could Rewind the Clock

Do you find yourself saying, *"I wish I could do that over again,"* or *"I feel so bad about what happened; I wish I had never said anything,"* or *"I wish I had never made that investment,"* or *"I wish I had never dated that person"*? When you make these kinds of statements you are living with regrets that can rob you of peace and happiness.

It's natural to want to turn back the clock and have the opportunity to do things differently. But I have come to the conclusion that "pushing rewind" to replay old events over and over again and wasting energy over past choices is not constructive. The fact is the past is behind us: it's over; it's history.

We would be wise to follow the wisdom of Alexander Graham Bell—that ingenious inventor who had many failed experiments before becoming famous.

> *When one door closes, another opens; but we often look*
> *so long and so regretfully upon the closed door that we*
> *do not see the one which has opened for us.*

I believe we would all live happier and more fulfilling lives if we stopped regretting the past. Instead, we should be thankful for who we are and the experiences we have had—both good and bad. It is through those experiences that we have become the person we are today.

I have made the decision to no longer wish I could turn back the clock and do something over. I focus on learning from each mistake I make and concentrate on making the changes I need in the future to become a better person. I draw from all my experiences to fulfill my purpose—to live a happy, healthy, and fulfilling life.

LTM Challenge

I challenge you to adopt my philosophy and follow my plan.

- Stop worrying about things you cannot change.
- Don't allow past experiences to drag you down.
- Accept yourself for you who are—blemishes and all.
- Learn from the past, enjoy the present, and plan for your future.
- Live your life with passion and purpose.

> **If we waste our time with regrets over yesterday,**
> **we will have no time to enjoy life today,**
> **or to make plans for tomorrow.**

97. The Missing LITTLE THING

Is there some area in your life where your performance doesn't meet your expectations? Would you like to know the Number 1 thing you can do that will bring about a significant improvement in that area? I truly believe there is one thing, particular to only you, that can make a big difference in your life.

Are You Like John?

John is a friend of mine from years ago, but his story is a perfect example of why it's important to consciously look for the LITTLE THING that's missing in our pursuit of success and happiness.

When it came to sales, John had everything going for him. He was disciplined and understood the importance of prospecting. He dressed like a successful salesman and was always on time for every appointment. He had all the necessary ingredients to succeed, except one. In business and social settings, John didn't know how to connect with people. As a result, he struggled and couldn't figure out what was holding him back. Likability was John's missing LITTLE THING.

All too often I see people, like John, who have tremendous potential but fall short of achieving their goals. They subconsciously ignore something that ultimately sabotages their success.

Obviously there are hundreds of LITTLE THINGS that play an important role in our success and relationships in life. It's all the LITTLE THINGS we do that when added together bring about significant changes in our lives.

However, as with any list, there's always one thing *unique to each one of us* that is going to make the greatest difference. Let's look at some illustrations:

- Joe, a loyal employee for six years, was an expert in his field. He met every requirement for the district manager position that just opened up. Unfortunately, he often ignored the company rules concerning business attire. This one thing kept him from being the candidate selected.

- Sue and Bob's marriage was struggling because Sue was not showing respect to Bob, and Bob ignored supplying what Sue needed. Neither saw his or her role in the unending cycle of withholding from one another.

- Diane and Jennifer both gave great presentations to a prospective client. The client liked both pitches equally but found that Diane's need to control every conversation was a turnoff. As a result, the client awarded the business to Jennifer.

If Joe, Sue, Bob, and Diane only knew what the missing LITTLE THING was that had defeated them, the outcome could have been different: a career advanced, a marriage saved, a sale made.

As is true in these examples, oftentimes it's just one thing that keeps us from taking a big step forward. What's the single biggest LITTLE THING that is holding you back in your career, or keeping you from building a better marriage, or having happier relationships with your friends or children?

When I was in sales, I called all the people who declined my services. I thanked them for giving me the opportunity to present. I told them I was committed to achieving my personal best and asked what I could have done differently to earn their business. It was a gold mine of advice, but one particular recommendation turned out to make the biggest difference. Because I was so focused on making the sale, I didn't take the time to show an elderly couple my genuine interest in the things that were important to them. By incorporating this one piece of feedback, my closing ratio was 100% with elderly home sellers.

LTM Challenge

I recommend two strategies to help you solve the mystery of your missing ingredient. These self-evaluation techniques may be the most demanding in this book, but the potential rewards can be life changing.

- **Reflect on your past.** Make a list of your unmet goals and disappointments. Before you say *"No thanks"* understand this is not an exercise intended to beat yourself up about the past. Rather, it's an opportunity for you to look for patterns in these situations and learn from them.

- **Ask for help.**   Enlist the help of a few trusted friends or colleagues. Ask them, *"What do you think is the one thing I could be doing differently to improve (my weak area)?"* Often the LITTLE THING we don't see is obvious to others, just as John's likability issue was clear to me.

Are you willing to figure it out?

> **You may be just one step away from solving your own mystery and breaking through the barrier that's holding you back.**

98. Become Your #1 Fan

Our self-image is largely influenced by the conversations we have with ourselves. Positive self-talk translates into positive self-esteem. Negative self-talk does just the opposite. If you aren't saying positive and encouraging things to yourself, it will be hard to have a good self-image. And YOU are the one in control of this internal dialogue.

While we often look to others for compliments and encouragement, it's really up to us to be our own cheerleaders. After all, how can we reasonably expect others to know and recognize all the little things we do each day to strive for our personal best? So if you are looking for encouragement, a high five, or a slap on the back, be prepared to fill those shoes yourself. We need to become our greatest fans and supporters.

If you chose to exercise even though you didn't feel like it, look in the mirror, smile and say to yourself, *"Great job!"*

If you have the propensity to make poor food choices, but today you made a good choice, tell yourself how happy you are about the decision you made.

If you have been going the extra mile to really listen to people and have not interrupted them, then congratulate yourself on your progress.

If you were proud of the way you handled a difficult situation, spend a few minutes to think about how you are growing as a person.

If you have just achieved a personal goal, do something you enjoy to celebrate.

If you are working on being more likable and you a leave conversation feeling like you really connected with the other person, say to yourself, "*Well done.*"

If being friendly is not natural for you, but today you pushed yourself to smile, made eye contact, and said "*Hi*" to the store clerk, reflect on the experience and encourage yourself to keep taking these baby steps each day.

If your co-workers are speaking poorly of someone and you withhold your comment even if you agree with them, be proud of your restraint.

Please understand that this is not about being conceited or egotistical. It's about acknowledging the good things you do and recognizing yourself to build your self-confidence.

LTM Challenge

If you struggle with a low self-image, write down everything you do in the course of a day that contributes to making you a better person. Carry a small note pad in your pocket, purse, or brief case.

If you pushed yourself outside your comfort zone to make a call you needed to make, write it down. If you took 30 minutes to read a good book rather than watching TV, write it down. If you smiled and answered the phone with a friendly voice, write it down. If you showed up for the meeting on time and well prepared, write it down.

Set a goal to make a list of at least 10 things a day that you are proud to have accomplished. If you will do this for one week, I guarantee that you will feel differently about yourself. You will have an improved attitude and be more content, confident, and inspired to work towards reaching your long-term goals.

Will you take me up on my challenge? Is your self-image important enough to make the effort for the next seven days?

> **If you look to others for words of encouragement**
> **and praise, you probably won't find them.**
> **Instead, look to yourself.**

99. Consistency Wins the Race

After being beaten by Tortoise, Hare reminded himself, *"Don't brag about your lightning pace, for Slow and Steady won the race!"*

There's wisdom for us in this age-old Aesop fable. In this lesson you'll discover the power of being consistent when it comes to reaching your goals.

Whether you have committed to eating healthier, exercising regularly, achieving an aggressive sales target, or building that savings account, being consistent plays a crucial role in achieving your goals.

Here's an example of what consistency can produce.

- A single penny doubled *every* day for 31 days results in a whopping $10,737,418.24.

- A single penny doubled *every other* day for 31 days yields just $163.84. That's less than 1/100th of 1 percent of the ten million you would get if you doubled it every day.

However, the real value of being consistent is not about how to make ten million dollars. Rather, it's about developing the persistence and patience necessary to stick with a goal until it is realized. Most people can push themselves to do something for a short time, but very few people will do the things they know they should do over an extended period of time.

What Are Your Consistency Zappers?

Be prepared to fight the consistency zappers—your excuses. Do any of these sound familiar?

- *"There are a million other things I have to deal with. It's impossible for me to focus on just one."* (It's too difficult.)

- *"It's hard for me to be consistent because I'm just so busy."* (I'm overwhelmed.)

- *"That project was important last week, but my priorities have shifted."* (I'm not in control.)

It's foolish to allow our excuses to sabotage us from the achievement of our goals. I have fought this battle of excuses enough during my career to know that the only way excuses won't present a challenge to consistency is if the goal you've identified is important enough.

Seven Ways to Increase Consistency

1. **Define the activities that drive results.** Select a goal you want to achieve. Then, block out an hour and put together a prioritized list of activities that, if performed correctly, will play a defining role in achieving your goal. These are the same activities you want to measure.

2. **Make a commitment**. After you identify the activities you need to do to accomplish your goals, make a commitment to do them consistently. Include the periods of time you will allocate to your activities.

3. **Don't allow excuses**. Resolve right now that you will not permit yourself to make excuses.

4. **Set up routines.** Establish a routine to do your daily activities. For example, if you are going to exercise every morning, allocate the amount of time you will need to do each activity up to and including your exercise period—such as getting out of bed, dressing, completing morning chores, and traveling to the gym.

5. **Take advantage of your peak energy state.** Figure out when your energy level is at its highest. It's much easier to do what you know you should do when you feel energetic rather than when you are exhausted.

6. **Do the challenging tasks first.** If the tasks that will drive your results and help you achieve your goal are difficult, do them first. It's easy to put off doing the things we don't enjoy.

7. **Review your goals often.** To help you be more consistent, review your goals each morning. It is the burning desire to achieve these goals that drives us to take action.

LTM Challenge

Is your goal important enough that you will commit to doing the correct activities daily for three weeks?

Psychologists tell us that it takes 21 days of daily repetition of a new behavior to make it a habit. So, what do you say? Will you do what you know you need to do for the next 21 days? Consistency will be easier once it becomes a habit for you.

> **You are in control of your life and how you spend your time.**
> **You can achieve any goal you set if**
> **you consistently do the LITTLE THINGS correctly.**

100. Persevere to Win

Achieving anything worthwhile requires a sustained effort over an extended period of time. Read the biographies of successful people and you won't find one who said the journey was quick and easy. The road to reaching your goals will be filled with roadblocks that require you to modify your course. You will experience pounding hailstorms that will beat the tar out of you and cause you to question whether your goal is worth the effort. People will fill your head with negative thoughts and tell you that you'll never make it. These are the reasons why there is little traffic on the road called "Going the Extra Mile."

Statistics for high-school dropouts are on the rise. Many college students, with good intentions, never receive a diploma. However, dropouts are not limited to students; we find them in many career fields today.

The fact is most people who set a goal to achieve something never follow through with their commitment. They start with the best of intentions but, when the time comes for them to do what is required to achieve their goal, they make excuses, justify their actions, and opt out.

Do you have what it takes to achieve a goal that is important to you? Are you the type of person who will hang in there long after the others have packed up and gone home?

Thomas Edison, the great inventor who failed thousands of times before he revolutionized the world by inventing the light bulb, summed it up perfectly: *"Our greatest weakness lies in giving up. The most certain way to succeed is always to try just one more time."*

If you are going to win, you must be mentally prepared to face your challenges head on. Accept the fact that it's not going to be easy. Be determined to fight through disappointments, failures, and times of discouragement. Recognize that patience is required because achieving anything worthwhile takes time. Most importantly, if you are giving your best and making measurable progress, don't allow yourself to give up.

Let's take a moment to consider your goals. What is the one goal that is most important to you? Is that goal important enough that you will stay the course and do what is required to win? When you get down and discouraged, are you strong enough to pick yourself up and go to the mat one more time?

Here is what I believe. You can achieve anything that is important to you if you are willing to go the extra mile required to succeed. The truth about success is that it is available to anyone who is willing to learn, remain disciplined, and persevere.

LTM Challenge

I challenge you to step up your game. Push harder than you have ever pushed yourself before. When you get down, remind yourself that everyone gets down at times, but the difference between you and many others is that you are a winner and not a quitter. Believe you are a winner and you will win.

> **When times get tough,
> the winners in life dig deep inside themselves
> to gather the strength to win.**

LTM Final Challenge

My ultimate goal in teaching the LITTLE THINGS is for you to recognize their importance and incorporate the *little-things-matter* way of thinking into your daily life. The LITTLE THINGS have universal applicability. Now I challenge you to start looking for and noticing the LITTLE THINGS you can do and say to achieve each of your personal goals. To help you in your quest, I invite you to read my blog posts, listen to the podcasts and download the free reports at LittleThingsMatter.com.

Parents—I challenge you to start looking for the LITTLE THINGS you can do to enhance your relationship with your children and be the example you want duplicated for future generations. Unless your children are unusual, they won't read this type of content without an incentive. I encourage you to offer each child an incentive to read this book. Imagine the results if your children incorporated these lessons into their daily lives.

Students—I challenge you to start working on these LITTLE THINGS right now. Your ultimate success and happiness will come from the compounding effect of the LITTLE THINGS you do. The sooner you get started working on yourself, the sooner you will achieve your personal and professional goals.

Employees—I challenge you to be the model employee every employer values. Treat your employer as your most valued customer. Make a list of 50 LITTLE THINGS you are committed to working on to grow your value to the market. Remember, income follows value.

Leaders—The people looking up to you are watching everything you do and noticing what you don't do. Remember, every LITTLE THING you do to get better will help your people get better as they duplicate your example. I challenge you to lead like never before. Make a list of at least 50 LITTLE THINGS you are committed to working on to become the type of leader people look up to with respect and admiration.

Business Owners—If you want your company to get better, you and your people must get better. It's that simple! Encourage, recognize, and invest in your people; help them achieve their personal best. Build a business culture that fosters growth and development. My challenge to you is to make a list of 50 LITTLE THINGS that will give your business the edge over your competitors.

Sales Professionals—I challenge you to step up your game. Be aggressive; make things happen. There is no limit to your earning potential, so go for it. Sit down and make a list of 50 LITTLE THINGS that you will work on in your pursuit to be the best at what you do. Once you finish with 50 LITTLE THINGS, continue adding more to your list. Start looking for every LITTLE THING you can do to improve your results.

Personal Favor—Do you know people who could benefit from reading this book? Will you please help me spread the word? Together we can make the world a better place for future generations. If there are people under your leadership, whether it is your children, grandchildren, employees, volunteers, or independent contractors, imagine the impact you could make on their lives if you gave them a copy of this book. For quantity discounts on this book and my expanded audio version, go to LittleThingsMatter.com/store. THANKS SO MUCH!

> **You can achieve anything that is important to you, if you do the LITTLE THINGS that matter!**

LITTLE THINGS MATTER
100 Ways to Improve Your Life Today!

Enhanced Audio Book Available

For the lessons in this book to have the greatest impact on your life, we recommend that you review them frequently. To help you implement these LITTLE THINGS into your daily life, the author has recorded this book on audio. The audio version includes extra insights, stories, and personal experiences not included in this hardback book. To purchase this audio program, go online to LittleThingsMatter.com/store.

Discounted Pricing

What more valuable gift could you give people than a book that will help them live a better life? Business owners, sales managers, community leaders and coaches: if you want your organization to get better, your people must get better. Special discounted pricing is available for bulk orders. Go online to LittleThingsMatter.com/store for bulk pricing.

More From Todd Smith

 To have Todd Smith's *Little Things Matter* lessons sent directly to your email Inbox, subscribe at LittleThingsMatter.com.

 Follow Todd's daily insights at Facebook.com/littlethingsmatter

 Follow Todd on Twitter at Twitter.com/toddsmith

 If you are interested in having Todd Smith speak at one of your upcoming events, he can be reached at todd@littlethingsmatter.com.